THE COMPASS
IN YOUR NOSE

THE COMPASS
IN YOUR NOSE

▼▼▼▼▼▼▼▼▼▼▼▼▼

And Other Astonishing
Facts about Humans

Marc McCutcheon

Illustrations by Rosanne Litzinger

JEREMY P. TARCHER, INC.
Los Angeles

Library of Congress Cataloging in Publication Data

McCutcheon, Marc.
   The compass in your nose and other astonishing facts about humans/
   Marc McCutcheon.
   p. cm.
   1. Anatomy, Human—Popular works. 2. Human physiology—Popular
   works. I. Title.
   QM26.M43 1989   89-34755
   612—dc20   CIP
   ISBN 0-87477-544-2

Jeremy P. Tarcher, Inc.
5858 Wilshire Blvd., Suite 200
Los Angeles, CA 90036

Distributed by St. Martin's Press, New York

Design by Tanya Maiboroda
Illustrations by Rosanne Litzinger

Manufactured in the United States of America
10 9 8 7 6 5 4 3 2 1

First Edition

To Mom, Dad, Deanna, and Dave

Contents

Part 4
OUR BEGINNING AND END

Acknowledgments

For research assistance, special thanks to Robin and Melanie Abendroth.

Thanks also to all of the following institutions for their contributions: Stanford University School of Medicine, Tufts University School of Medicine, George Washington University Medical School, Case Western Reserve University, University of Massachusetts Medical Center, University of Colorado Health Sciences Center, University of Texas Health Science Center, Penn State University, Emory University School of Medicine, University of California at Los Angeles and San Diego, Duke University Medical Center, and University of Miami School of Medicine.

Introduction

Within the darker reaches of the human body lies a museum. There are artifacts there. Dusty. Moldy. Cobwebbed. Left behind by our ancestors eons ago not in haste, but through a delicate process known as *natural selection*. Chip through the patina of the ages and these artifacts will appear. Little genetic diary notes. Faded scribblings of secret codes. Scary and wonderful mementos from deep within our grandmother's evolutionary hope chest.

Near the neck of a developing human embryo, for example, close to where a smiling face will soon form, are two strange and beautiful holes on either side, looking distinctly primordial.

Gill pouches. Not lung sacs. Not eye sockets. Gill pouches.

In early stages of development, these pouches are virtually identical to those in a fish embryo, and all mammals, not just humans, have them. In fishes, the pouches become functional gills. In humans, they grow into something quite different: they are genetically reprogrammed to form the skeleton of the larynx and the muscles of the face.

On rare occasions the old coding that produces these vestigial pouches conjures up a more tantalizing reminder of the past and in the process scares everyone half to death. A case in point was a 9-year-old girl who had "horns" growing out of both sides of her neck. *Science News* reported that the horns were probably the remnants of gills: "During the early stages of pre-birth development, human babies have gills like a fish. Sometimes when these gills disappear, as the embryo develops, cysts grow where the gills were. When the cysts remain after the baby is born, they look like small horns."

The girl's horns were surgically removed; they were each about half an inch long. It was discovered that her mother had also had them, as did many of the females in the girl's family. In fact, the horns could be traced back as far as five generations. Such "ancestral reminiscence" is nature's way of reminding us where we've been and how far we've come.

Under the framework of evolution, new foundations are laid on top of old foundations. Recapitulation, the theory that the embryo repeats or recapitulates the old stages our ancestors followed through natural selection, was first proposed by the nineteenth-century German anatomist Ernst Haeckel and has passed through several periods of acceptance and damnation ever since.

There's also the lanugo, the downy coat of fur that the fetus grows at six months. In *The Descent of Man* Charles Darwin wrote: "[Lanugo] is first developed on the eyebrows and face, and especially 'round the mouth, where it is much longer than that on the head." Like the embryonic tail, the lanugo disappears before birth, except in extremely rare cases. *Hypertrichopherosis* is the medical term for the superabundance of body and facial hair sometimes found on newborns.

The recapitulating womb isn't the only place to find artifacts, however. The adult human body is a walking testament to our evolutionary heritage. The vermiform appendix, for example, which corresponds to the cecum in grazing animals, once helped our ancestors digest grass and vegetable cellulose. The function of this lymph-filled sack today, however, is unknown.

Equally mysterious is the disappearance of the rhinarium, a strip of moist flesh that hung down from the noses of our ancestors to help them smell. The rhinarium is still found in most wet-snouted animals. In humans, the two vertical ridges that connect the upper lip and the nose are all that remain of this ancient organ.

Most humans still have a trace amount of iron in the lining of our noses, a rudimentary compass that aids in directional finding relative to the earth's magnetic field. Unlike many animals, such as dolphins, pigeons, and honeybees, it appears humans have forgotten how to use this fabulous sixth sense.

The human museum is full of fascinating artifacts like these. Smile and you utilize muscles originally designed for snarling. Raise your eyebrows and you use the remnant of a muscle intended eons ago to "twitch" the skin, as many animals still do today. Wiggle your ears and you demonstrate in a rudimentary way the ear-cocking ability of our predator-wary forebears.

In addition, there's blood serum that is 99 percent identical to seawater . . . fingernails fine-tuned from claws . . . canine teeth with unusually deep root systems . . . vanishing molars . . . muscles to raise the hackles. . . . The museum is always open, its fossils always on display.

The body is also a temple, warehouse, laboratory, pharmacy (the brain alone produces more than 50 psychoactive drugs), electric company, farm, mass-transit system, library (the brain stores the equivalent information of 500 sets of the *Encyclopaedia Britannica*), utility company, hospital, and sewage treatment plant. It also has a self-regulating police force, with daily infusions of millions of microscopic criminals and terrorists to apprehend; an array of traffic controllers; an army of medics and mechanics (a trillion platelets cruise the circulatory system daily in search of wounds); centralized and outlying governments that argue with one another (the stomach and the brain, for example, never agree on taking that second helping of chocolate cake); and motors, pumps, compressors, vacuums, regulators, air conditioners, furnaces, plumbing, filters, strainers, thermostats, alarm clocks, timers, and more.

The body builds itself from a single cell into an assemblage of over 100 trillion cells. It then questions its own existence with statements such as, "I think, therefore I am" (René Descartes). It is self-aware: "A cell state in which every cell is a citizen" (Rudolf Virchow). It is self-deprecating: "A hodge-podge of sagging livers, sinking gall bladders, drooping stomachs, compressed intestines, and squashed pelvic organs" (John Button). It is tortured by imperfection: "The organ of the accumulated smut and sneakery of 10,000 generations of weaseling souls" (Philip Wylie). It is thoughtful: "Nevertheless, it is even harder for the ape to believe that he has descended from man" (Henry Mencken).

Samuel Butler saw the human *body* as a "pair of pincers set over a bellows and a stewpan, the whole fixed upon stilts." The human *being,* however, is so much more than that. Beyond the portable plumbing, the altered fish, and the renovated ape is the metamorphosized flame of the universe itself. We are, after all, evolved comets and sunbeams. From stardust we are born, and to stardust we will return.

The human form, said Joseph Addison, is a system "fitted to another after so wonderful a manner as to make a proper engine for the soul to work with." And that, hopefully, is what this book is all about: not a dry, academic rendering of the anatomy, but a childlike scrutiny of an anatomy of wonder. The human angel, ape, and fish. The astonishing machine that evolution has built. The temple that took over 4 billion years to perfect.

The lion is stronger, the monkey a better climber, the deer swifter, and the potato, incredibly, more genetically complex. Yet no other creation of nature fascinates us quite as much as ourselves. So it is that we indulge our self-absorption once more in yet another volume about our favorite subject: humans.

Human Chronology

4.2 BILLION YEARS AGO

The Spreading of Life
The earth's clouds of hydrogen, carbon monoxide, ammonia, and methane generate fierce electrical storms over the seas. Bathed in the sun's ultraviolet rays, the gases interact and form complex molecules—including sugars, nucleic acids, and amino acids—that pave the way for the development of proteins and self-replicating DNA. After a few million years, single-cell bacteria, the simplest life forms, colonize the seas. The evolution of life begins.

3.5 BILLION YEARS AGO

Oxygen
Blue-green algae disperses the first breaths of oxygen into the atmosphere. The oxygen serves to block the sun's dangerous ultraviolet rays, allowing new species to evolve. It is the single most important element in the history of life.

1

900 MILLION YEARS AGO

First Primitive Sponges
Sponges are among the first simple, multicellular animals to evolve from single-cell life.

570 MILLION YEARS AGO

Mollusks
The most intelligent of the mollusks are the octopus and the squid, which are thought to have evolved from the shelled nautilus at this time.

540 MILLION YEARS AGO

First Fish
The first fish are jawless filter feeders with circular mouths. Small and finless, they resemble today's lamprey.

440 MILLION YEARS AGO

First Mass Extinction
Mass extinction of sea life. Many species mysteriously vanish from the face of the earth, never to return.

415 MILLION YEARS AGO

First Ferns

Club mosses, giant horsetails, and ferns are among the first plants to grow tall and overshadow other plants to gain more sunlight. Some grow as high as 90 feet, but only the ferns develop the first true leaves.

Buried and compacted in the earth, these plants will be dug up as coal by man hundreds of millions of years later.

375 MILLION YEARS AGO

First Amphibians

Some fish develop specialized air sacs to help them breathe in swampy areas low in oxygen. The air sacs eventually become lungs, allowing animals to leave the water and live on land. The amphibians are first to develop eardrums and vocal cords.

3

340 MILLION YEARS AGO

First Insects
The fossil record reveals some insects of unnerving dimensions: foot-long cockroaches and dragonflies with 30-inch wingspans.

320 MILLION YEARS AGO

Reptiles: The Forerunners of Dinosaurs
Crocodiles, lizards, tortoises, and turtles have evolved from amphibians. They and many of their fellow reptiles will survive the climate changes destined to destroy the dinosaurs and will remain largely unchanged over the eons.

270 MILLION YEARS AGO

Trees
Pines, larches, cedars, and firs evolve from ferns and other primitive plants and eventually overshadow them.

250 MILLION YEARS AGO

Second Mass Extinction
The dawn of a 20-million-year ice age when mass extinction occurs: 96 percent of all animal species are wiped out. An estimated 75 percent of amphibian families and 80 percent of reptile families vanish entirely, never to return.

225 MILLION YEARS AGO

Age of the Dinosaurs
Earth's spin has been slowing for millions of years, lengthening the hours in a day, while shortening the number of days in a year. At the beginning of the dinosaur age there are 385 days in a year, due to the earth's faster rotation. By the time their reign ends, the year will dwindle to just 371 days.

Shrews and micelike creatures are the largest mammals alive at the advent of the dinosaur age.

174 MILLION YEARS AGO

Primitive Birds
The scales of some reptiles mutate and evolve into rudimentary feathers. The first primitive birds take flight.

139 MILLION YEARS AGO

First Flowers

Plants evolve flowers to attract insects through color and scent. The insects cross-fertilize other plants with collected pollen, allowing both plants and insects to thrive and evolve further.

Magnolias and water lilies are the first true flowers.

74 MILLION YEARS AGO

First Primates

The primitive ancestors of man, the prosimians, are the first creatures with the ability to "grasp" objects in their hands.

70 MILLION YEARS AGO

Largest Flying Creatures

The largest flying creature ever known, the pterosaur, glides over what is now the state of Texas. Remains discovered in Big Bend National Park in 1971 indicate that the reptile weighed 200 pounds and boasted a wingspan close to 40 feet. Incidentally, crocodiles living in Big Bend during this time grew as long as 52 feet.

50 MILLION YEARS AGO

Primates Spread

Lemurs and other prosimians thrive in Madagascar, Europe, and North America.

37 MILLION YEARS AGO

First Apes Swing from the Trees
The apes—chimps, gorillas, gibbons, and orangutans—branch off from old-world monkeys, developing larger and more complex brains and skeletal changes that allow them more freedom to walk upright. Their arms rotate 180 degrees, allowing hand-over-hand brachiation between tree limbs.

Meanwhile, the largest land mammal of all time roams Asia and Europe. Baluchitherium—a hornless, long-necked, treetop-eating rhino—stands 18 feet high at the shoulder and weighs 33 tons.

6 TO 10 MILLION YEARS AGO

Evolution of Humans
The human lineage begins to diverge from chimps and gorillas. Even today our genes are 98 percent identical to chimpanzees.

5 MILLION YEARS AGO

Australopithecus Afarensis

The oldest fossils belonging to one of our earliest direct ancestors, the *Australopithecus,* were unearthed in 1984 by a joint expedition from Harvard University and the National Museum of Kenya near Lake Baringo in northern Kenya. A two-inch-long fragment of its lower jaw with two molar teeth was found among fossil pigs and elephants and is similar to the famed "Lucy" fossils discovered earlier in Ethiopia. The remains indicate that this South African "ape man" weighed less than 80 pounds, stood just 57 inches high, and could probably outrun many of his four-footed contemporaries.

1.5 MILLION YEARS AGO

Homo Erectus Migrates to Asia and Europe

Due to their ability to control fire, *Homo erectus* was the first to migrate to colder climates. They greatly improved the toolmaking skills of their ancestors. The first hand ax, for example, originated with *erectus.* The use of rudimentary language may have begun during this period as well.

Homo erectus lived in a world vastly alien to the one we know today. Not only was the climate different—the worldwide average temperature hovered around 95°F—but man's neighborhood was also exceedingly strange.

In East Africa, gargantuan versions of modern mammals dominated the landscape. A tusked pig as large as a rhinoceros (paleontologists who discovered their remains originally thought the tusks belonged to elephants) was a typical example of the bizarre, overgrown creatures *erectus* may have hunted— or tried desperately to avoid.

An early breed of sheep stood seven feet tall. Unlike today's sheep, they sported horns that would span the length of a midsize automobile. The baboons of the day were no laughing matter, either. They were doubtless as ferocious as our modern short-tempered baboons, but with one frightening difference: they were as big as gorillas.

Even more formidable was an ape-like "thing" living in the Far East at the time. When its fossils were first discovered, scientists believed it to be a giant human and named it *Gigantopithecus*. Later analysis, however, revealed the behemoth to be little more than an advanced, overgrown ape, standing up to 9 feet tall and tipping the scales at 600 pounds. Its molars— six times broader than our own—were once sold by Chinese druggists as "dragon's teeth" and were often ground into medicines.

And then, of course, there were the incredibly huge brutes: the mammoths. Their frozen carcasses are still found in parts of Siberia today—flesh intact and, on one occasion, actually eaten by twentieth-century man. The mammoths and mastodons were the largest land mammals man has ever seen.

80,000 YEARS AGO

Neanderthal Man Inhabits the North
Erroneously viewed as a dim-witted, savage ogre, the Neanderthals were the first in the human lineage to show reverence to the dead. In the Zagros Mountains of Iraq, remains of

an ancient burial were discovered. At the gravesite, remains of assorted flowers—with known medicinal properties—were found carefully arranged around a Neanderthal man from 60,000 years ago. A pollen analysis revealed that the arrangement consisted of yarrow, cornflower, St. Barnaby's thistle, ragwort, grape hyacinth, hollyhock, and woody horsetail.

40,000 TO 60,000 YEARS AGO

Cro-Magnon Man Originates Art and Advanced Tools

Cro-Magnons are credited with the following inventions: bow and arrow, harpoon, fueled lamp, sewing needle, tailored leggings and tunics, collared shirts and cuffed sleeves, and art.

Shunning caves, Cro-Magnon man preferred to build shelters of wood, stone, bone (mammoth bones were sometimes used for framing), and skins. In some parts of the world, our ancestors killed giant armadillos, stripped them of their Volkswagen-sized shells, and used them for temporary shelters. To take advantage of solar heating, most Cro-Magnon homes were deliberately constructed facing south. Stone hearths were used for additional heating as well as for cooking. These cozy homes even boasted wall-to-wall carpeting made of soft animal pelts. Later homes had interior lighting—stone lamps fueled by fat and moss wicks.

Although the maximum life span for Neanderthal man was age 45, Cro-Magnons lived longer, with a few individuals surviving to age 60 or 65. Leading causes of death probably included starvation, deficiency diseases, infections, injuries (though like Neanderthals, Cro-Magnons took great pains to care for their invalid), intense cold, and predator attacks.

50,000 YEARS AGO

First Seaworthy Boats
The fossil record shows that humans made the first sea crossing to Australia at this time.

30,000 TO 40,000 YEARS AGO

Modern Humans
Humans evolved in present-day anatomy and behavior. The use of complex language likely originated during this critical period, because the archeological record reveals an explosion of innovations and inventions, a clear testimony to improved communication.

The last of the Neanderthals are thought to have died out during this period.

18,000 YEARS AGO

Ice Age Peaks
Ice is more than a mile thick over Boston. The world is covered with ice as far south as New York and London.

10,000 TO 15,000 YEARS AGO

Farming Begins

Our ancestors begin domestication of animals. Sheep had little wool before humans bred them, and chickens laid eggs only seasonally. Wild cows produced milk only when nursing their young.

Later, the invention of the microlith (sickle) and grinding stone opened up the harvesting and processing of large tracts of wild grain, paving the way for radical changes in economic, social, and political systems. Early bands of humans were now ready to abandon their migratory way of life for agriculture.

11,000 YEARS AGO

First Cities

The largest city on earth, Chemi Shanidar in Iraq, is popu-lated with just 150 people.

5,000 YEARS AGO

Human civilization begins
in earnest.

TWENTIETH
CENTURY
YOU ARE HERE!

PART
1

OUR
INFINITE
VARIETY

▼▼▼▼▼▼▼▼▼▼▼▼▼

Our
Numbers

OUR OVERBURDENED PLANET

Until the 1960s, most countries of the world shared a "pronatalist" philosophy—that is, population growth was encouraged because it was thought to strengthen a nation's economy.

Few nations maintain such a philosophy today, however, because unmanageable populations so frequently go hand-in-hand with economic disaster. Huge populations not only strain a nation's resource bank but also leave them more vulnerable to a host of other catastrophes, including famine, epidemics, war, and even deleterious acts of nature. As living space runs out, increasing numbers of people are forced into hazardous areas, such as earthquake and flood zones. In 1970 a cyclone generated a tidal wave that killed 300,000 people in Bangladesh. The disaster occurred again in 1984, killing tens of thousands more.

Many experts believe the earth already has more humans than it can safely maintain. Although worldwide pollution and its environmental consequences have already grown beyond manageable proportions, the worst is yet to come if projections of new automobiles on the road in developing nations are any indication.

Equally disturbing is the rapid loss of wildlife. By the year

2000, about 100 different species of plants and animals will suffer extinction each day as humans continue to gobble up the last remaining tracts of habitable land.

Most modern nations are moving closer to the goal of equilibrium between birthrates and death rates, with some European countries already experiencing zero or below zero population growth.

The governments of most developing nations, meanwhile, have initiated massive birth-control programs, making sex education and contraceptives widely available at low or no cost to its citizens. Experts, however, say growth is so out-of-control in many of these nations that the goal of zero population growth may not be attained for nearly a century.

How Many Humans?

Within one minute after you read the first word of this sentence, 160 babies will be born. Of these, 50 will be born in India, another 34 will grow up Chinese, and 11 more will one day become Soviets.

Now look at your watch again. Count off two seconds. Somewhere on earth a child has just died. A child dies, in fact, with every breath you take. Every two seconds. Twenty-four hours a day. Of the children born this year alone, 17 million will not live to see their fifth birthday.

Count off five minutes more. Now 300 men, women, and children are gone.

How did they die? A striking proportion perished by starvation and malnutrition-related diseases, to which a staggering overall death count of 50 million has been attributed yearly.

Yet the population of the world continues to swell by an additional 250,000 human beings every day, or approximately 90,000,000 per year. At the end of each year, enough new people arrive to populate the equivalent of 12½ New York cities. Demographers believe the world's population must stabilize—from sheer necessity—at 10 to 15 billion during the next century.

16

Meanwhile, human life spans are lengthening, further increasing our already swollen populace. In 1750 America, the typical life span was 40. Today most Americans can expect to survive well into their seventies and beyond. Scientists believe it may some day be possible to short-circuit the aging process altogether so that humans may survive indefinitely.

By the year 3530, if the population were to increase at its present rate, the total weight of human beings would equal the weight of the earth.

Total Humans in the History of the Earth

If no one had died in the last 600,000 years, the earth today would be overrun with more than 80 billion human beings.

Babies Booming

In March of 1987 the earth officially welcomed aboard its 5 billionth human passenger. The following countries led the world with new births:

India—52.4 births per minute (pop. 816,800,000). India is currently trying to create a family "norm" of two children by the turn of the century. The government has even offered cash payments to citizens who undergo voluntary sterilization. India's population has already reached crisis proportions. One-tenth of Calcutta's populace, for example, are homeless and live and sleep in the streets. The country's population, meanwhile, is nearing the billion mark.

China—34.3 births per minute (pop. 1,087,000,000). China is trying to limit its population growth to 1 percent per year by urging couples to have only one child. One-child families receive subsidy and priority housing incentives, while two-child families lose these benefits. In some areas of China, the parents of a third child are fined 10 percent of their income until the child reaches 14 years of age. Consequently, infanticide—particularly of females—is rampant, as are community-mandated late-term abortions.

The population crisis in China is so critical that it even affects the dead: the government is now urging cremation for the deceased because the country is running out of land for burial grounds.

USSR—10.9 births per minute (pop. 286,000,000). Frequent food shortages and long waiting lists for appliances and automobiles testify to the Soviets' strained system of supply and demand. Even in the most heavily forested area in the world, the Soviets often must do without vital paper products, such as toilet paper. The Soviet attempt to manage its population, however, is heavily frustrated by a scarcity of contraceptives, which has made abortion the most widely used form of birth control.

Nigeria—10.3 births per minute (pop. 112,000,000). Nigeria is black Africa's most densely populated nation. In the next 30 years its population will soar from 112 million to 274 million, making it one of the fastest-growing countries on earth. Lagos, its largest city, increased its population from

329,000 in 1952 to over 7 million today.

The Nigerian government is currently spending over $100 million to make contraceptives and sex education available to everyone. Contraceptive use among women has increased from 2 percent in 1983 to 6 percent today.

United States—7.9 births per minute (population 246,100,000). Economics alone is forcing couples to have fewer children. Although early in the century couples thought five children to be an easily managed flock, Americans now consider a two-children family to be ideal.

The United States receives more immigrants each year than any other nation. More than 52 million immigrants have become legal U.S. citizens in the last 165 years; meanwhile, 1 in every 24 today is an *illegal* immigrant.

Egypt—7.5 births per minute (pop. 53,300,000). Egypt's population is now increasing at a rate of 1 million every 10 months. The total population, approximately 26 million in the 1960s, has now soared to more than 50 million in a country of which nearly 94 percent is uninhabitable desert.

Housing has become so scarce in Egypt that hundreds of thousands of citizens have been forced to take up residence in the tombs and mausoleums of a huge Islamic cemetery (City of the Dead) outside Cairo.

Islam, the nation's major religion, accepts birth control but forbids abortion.

Pakistan—6.8 births per minute (pop. 107,500,000). Three million Afghan refugees have swelled Pakistan's populace since the onset of the Soviet/Afghan war in 1980. Pakistan is projected to double its population of 107 million to 214 million in 30 years. Its largest city, Karachi, will have more than 12 million people by the turn of the century.

Bangladesh—6.2 births per minute (pop. 109,500,000). Nearly 110 million people currently live in an area the size of Arkansas, and the population is projected to reach 206 million in 30 years.

Our Drain on Resources

The typical American now directly or indirectly consumes 20 tons of minerals a year in such various forms as new pavement, concrete, glass, oil, coal, and metal. The rate at which we've mined minerals has doubled every ten years.

According to environmentalists, the world demand for water is quickly outstripping supply. By the year 2000, population growth alone will double the demand for water in half the countries of the world.

Although the United States receives 4,200 billion gallons of rainfall each day, water tables have dropped dramatically in many parts of the West in the last several years due to skyrocketing consumption. In 1900, Americans used 40 billion gallons of water per day. By 1980, we were consuming some 700 billion gallons daily.

The Most and the Fewest

The earth still has many areas left where human inhabitants are few and far between, while other locations are so crowded there is scarcely breathing room. Two of the least crowded areas, due to their massive ice sheets and cold climates, are Kalaallit Nunaat (formerly Greenland) and Antarctica. The following locations—listed from most sparsely to most densely habitated—reflect this diverse range:

1. *Antarctica.* Maximum population at any one time is 2,000, most of which are visiting scientists. With its 6,000,000 miles of land mass, population density is 1 person per 3,000 square miles.
2. *Kalaallit Nunaat (Greenland).* 1 person per 15 square miles.
3. *Falkland Islands.* The land averages less than ½ a human per square mile. Sheep outnumber people here by three to one.
4. *Mongolia.* 3 people per square mile.

5. ***Australia.*** 5 people per square mile.
6. ***Canada.*** 7 people per square mile.
7. ***United States.*** The United States still boasts huge tracts of uninhabited land, particularly in the western deserts and in Alaska. The country averages a modest 68 humans per square mile.
8. ***China.*** 294 people per square mile.
9. ***India.*** 664 people per square mile.
10. ***Japan.*** 854 people per square mile.
11. ***Bangladesh.*** This is the most densely populated non-island region in the world, with 1,969 humans per square mile. Here, 110 million people live in an area the size of the state of Arkansas.
12. ***Macau.*** This island off the coast of China is a sardine can of tightly packed humans, with an incredible 63,000 people per square mile. It is the most densely populated territory on earth.

The Eye of the Beholder
According to studies of human attractiveness, 8 percent of the world's population is considered extremely good looking; 17 percent better than average; 50 percent average; 17 percent somewhat below average; and 8 percent ugly.

The beautiful people of the world enjoy certain advantages. In studies of the value of good looks in society, the following has been discovered:

- On an attractiveness scale of 1 to 10, people rated a "3" by researchers earned an average income of $10,000; those rated a "6" earned between $10,000 and $20,000; and people who received the highest rating earned more than $20,000 per year.
- Attractive waitresses are given 5 percent larger tips than less attractive ones.
- Hospital emergency staff are significantly more likely to try to revive DOAs (dead on arrival) who are considered good-looking than those who are not.
- Tall people are given far more positions of power than short people.
- Women with large breasts are considered by both sexes to be less competent than women with small breasts.

INTO THE YEAR 2000

Twelve thousand years ago the world population totaled a mere 5 million people; today it has escalated to more than 5 billion; in less than one century that total will more than double again to 10 billion men, women, and children.

A Chronology of Population

Date	Global Population
10,000 B.C.	5,000,000
1 A.D.	200,000,000
1000	275,000,000
1500	420,000,000
1700	615,000,000

1900	1,625,000,000
1920	1,862,000,000
1940	2,295,000,000
1960	3,049,000,000
1975	4,033,000,000
1980	4,432,000,000
1988	5,128,000,000
2000	6,200,000,000
2033	8,700,000,000

(China alone will have more than 1,516,000,000 people in 2033, almost the population of the entire world in 1900. India will have 1,311,000,000. Their combined population will be nearly equivalent to the population of the world in 1960.)

Big City Blues

The largest human populations 3,000 years ago could be found in three cities, two located in the river valleys of the Nile, and one located on the banks of the Tigris and Euphrates rivers to the east. In Egypt, 100,000 humans crowded together in the city of Thebes, while another 74,000 swelled the population of Memphis. Farther east, about 50,000 made their home in the thriving metropolis of Babylon.

Even 1,000 years later the largest city on earth, Rome, had only 600,000 people. Late in the eighteenth century, Peking was the first city to exceed 1 million inhabitants.

Today cities with populations of 1 million or more have become exceedingly common.

By the year 2000, in fact, Mother Earth will have 440 urban areas with populations over 1 million. Of these, 191 will have 2 million humans each. An additional 82 population centers will boast nearly 4 million residents.

These include:

1. Mexico City, 26 million
2. São Paulo, 24 million

3. Tokyo, 17 million
4. Calcutta, 17 million
5. Bombay, 16 million
6. New York/Northeast New Jersey, 15.5 million
7. Seoul, 13.5 million
8. Shanghai, 13.5 million
9. Rio de Janeiro, 13.3 million
10. Delhi, 13.3 million
11. Buenos Aires, 13.2 million
12. Cairo, 13.2 million
13. Jakarta, 12.8 million
14. Bagdad, 12.8 million
15. Tehran, 12.7 million
16. Karachi, 12.2 million
17. Istanbul, 11.9 million
18. Los Angeles/Long Beach, 11.2 million
19. Dacca/Bangladesh, 11.2 million
20. Manila, 11.1 million

The implications of these population projections are indeed staggering. If present trends continue, we see that the most crowded urban area in the year 2000 will be Mexico City, with 26 million human inhabitants. But Mexico City already has more than a quarter of a million homeless.

Furthermore, Mexico City's daily production of garbage is unrivaled anywhere. Every day some 9,000 tons of human-generated garbage is left to pile up on sidewalks for days or weeks before finally being carted off.

Indeed, by the year 2000 Mexico City will likely be the earth's dirtiest, most polluted urban area, with a projected 6 million automobiles on the road. Unless drastic measures are taken soon, the city authorities will be forced to set up emergency oxygen supplies for pedestrians overcome by toxic fumes. (Tokyo has already taken this measure, due to its own pollution problem.)

Our
Racial
Stocks

HOW WE DIFFER

There are, generally speaking, three main types of humans in the world: Caucasoid (55 percent of world population); Mongoloid (33 percent); and Negroid (8 percent).

Contrary to what these figures may imply, every human on earth is a progeny of Africa—that is, we all come from Negroid stock. Whites and Asians are actually late additions to the human lineage.

Each of the three main types of races we know today is physically different from the other and instantly recognizable. But why the variations? Why don't all humans look alike?

The answer is a simple matter of climate and survival of the fittest. The Eskimo serves as a perfect illustrative example of how environmental factors caused races to become distinct from one another.

Fat

Fat is an excellent insulator against the cold, and the Eskimos have developed more of it than any other people. The average Eskimo, in fact, weighs about 170 pounds.

In contrast, the warmer the climate, the less need for body

fat. The average Irishman—who evolved in a warmer climate—weighs 157 pounds. The typical Spaniard, who enjoys an even warmer climate, weighs 132 pounds. At the extreme end of the scale, meanwhile, is the Algerian Berber, reared in the desert heat and typically weighing in at just 125 pounds.

Body Shape

The less body surface exposed to the environment, the greater the conservation of body heat. The shape of the Eskimo body varies widely from natives of hotter climates; their stature is stockier, with shorter hands, arms, and legs, larger chests, longer torsos, and rounder heads. By contrast, the lean, long-limbed bodies of tropical natives have a high surface-to-volume ratio, which more efficiently radiates heat.

Metabolism

Metabolism consists of the whole complex of bodily processes that occur in the interchange of materials between a living organism and its environment. The higher the metabolic rate, the higher the threshold for sensing cold. The Eskimo's metabolic rate is 15 to 30 percent higher than the European's. Equatorial people have the lowest metabolism of all because fewer calories need to be burned to keep their bodies warm. Consequently, a Brazilian visiting Alaska will suffer from cold much more intensely than the Eskimo natives.

Blood Flow

The greater the blood flow to the skin, the greater its capacity to resist frostbite and the effects of prolonged cold. Every pound of additional fat creates an extra 200 miles of blood capillaries throughout the body. One study showed that some Eskimos produce twice as much blood flow to the hands as white men, which may be due to their heavier fat ratio.

Eyes and Nose

Dark skin and folded eyelids serve as a shield against sunlight, which is most intense when reflected off snow and sand. Eskimos, other Mongoloids, and Negroids who originated in sunnier climates possess these characteristics while Caucasoids do not. A flattened nose—characteristic of the Eskimo—exposes less area to the cold and is less likely to suffer frostbite.

Senses

As a rule, the people who live in the most primitive environments enjoy the best-developed senses. The Eskimo, for example, can detect odors far more acutely than Caucasians. They also have better color vision: only 1 percent of the male Eskimo population is color blind, compared to 8 percent of Caucasians and 5 percent of Asians.

The African Bushman, meanwhile, boasts both superior hearing and eyesight. The typical Bushman, in fact, can make out four moons of Jupiter without the use of a telescope and can hear the sound of an approaching airplane from as far as 70 miles away.

Body Hair

Caucasoids have the most hair and Mongoloids the least. The Eskimo has the fewest body hairs of all; many even lack pubic hair. It is not known why Eskimos share this characteristic.

OTHER PHYSICAL DIFFERENCES BETWEEN RACES

Some anthropologists maintain that the human lineage can be broken down into no less than 4,000 individual races. Others go further and cite more than 5 billion individual races—that is, every human is his or her own distinct "race" because obvious differences can be found in virtually every individual on the planet.

Despite our differences, the races are actually much more closely related than was once thought. For example, there are actually more variations between some American blacks and blacks of other nations than there are between American blacks and American whites. Australian aborigines, for instance, are thought to be closer in lineage to whites than blacks overall, even though their skin color would appear to indicate otherwise.

All things considered, the similarities between races vastly outnumber the differences, which makes the concept of prejudice nothing more than a judgment against members of our own family circle. Without losing sight of the overall value of mankind's commonality, then, we can now more objectively examine some of the distinguishing features of our varying racial stocks.

Skin

The pigmentation in our skin serves as protection from the sun's ultraviolet rays. In areas where sunlight is intense, humans have evolved darker skin for greater protection against harmful ultraviolet rays. In other regions, where the duration and intensity of sunlight is lower, less skin pigment is necessary. Thus evolves the wide variation of skin tones, from white to yellow, brown to black.

Varying skin tones also help in the regulation of vitamin D formation, the main source of which is sunlight. Too much Vitamin D causes kidney disease; too little causes rickets.

The yellow skin of the Eskimo contains a layer of keratin that helps regulate exposure to sunlight in snowy or desert regions.

Ear Wax

One of the most accurate ways to distinguish Asians from blacks and whites is to check for differences in ear wax (see the table below). Asians produce dry, crumbly ear wax; whites and blacks produce a moist, adhesive wax.

Lineage	Percentage with Dry Ear Wax
Northern Chinese	98
Southern Chinese	86
Japanese	92
Micronesians	61
Germans	18
American whites	16
American blacks	7

Finger and Hair Whorls

Orientals have more finger whorls than whites or blacks, who in turn have more loops. Australian aborigines have the most whorls of any people. An estimated 80 percent of Europeans have hair that whorls counterclockwise at the back of the head. Most Japanese hair, however, goes in the opposite direction.

Teeth

Mongoloids tend to have shovel-shaped incisors; whites and blacks, in contrast, have chisel-shaped ones. Asians frequently have either impacted or missing wisdom teeth, whereas the Australian aborigine has an extra set of molars that no one else on earth has. In addition, aborigine teeth are also the largest of all humans.

Brain Size

Scientists as yet have not found that brain size makes any measurable difference in intelligence. Neanderthal man, in fact, had a larger brain than modern man. Consider as well the difference between men and women: men have larger brains, yet women score higher on IQ tests.

The Kaffirs and the Amahosa of Africa actually have larger brains than Caucasoids, as do the Japanese, the American Indians, the Eskimos, and the Mongols.

Blood

Mountain dwellers' blood is richer in hemoglobin and their hearts and chests are larger in order to process the thinner oxygen supply found at high altitudes. Lowlanders who visit the mountains typically experience fatigue, insomnia, headaches, stomach cramps, rapid pulse, and chronic dehydration—a reaction termed *mountain sickness*—as a result of decreased oxygen intake.

The most common blood type among Europeans and North Americans is type O, followed in order of prevalence by type A, type B, and type AB. Aborigines and Eskimos are evenly split between type O and type A, while the Japanese have the highest rate (11 percent of the population) of AB blood, a trait they share with the Egyptians.

Height

The tallest human tribe on earth is the Tutsi of Central Africa. Tutsi grow as tall as seven feet, with the average height slightly over six feet. The shortest humans are the pygmies, who stop growing at the age of ten due to a lack of growth hormone. Pygmy males average only four feet, six inches. Following in height are the Scottish, the Australian aborigines, and some North American Indians. Following in shortness are the Lapps of Scandinavia, the American Indians of Labrador, the Negritos of Southeast Asia, and some Asiatic Indians.

Scent

Each of us has our very own distinguishing odor. Deprived of sight and sound, Helen Keller developed the ability to identify each of her friends by smell alone. In fact, even races smell different to other races. Diet plays an important role in how we smell. Consequently, Americans could conceivably smell like butter to the Japanese, and the Japanese could conceivably smell like fish to Americans.

Equally significant is the distribution of apocrines, specialized scent glands located throughout the genital, anal, and underarm regions that send out the scent signals we know as body odor. In general, the greater the quantity of apocrines, the stronger the smell that results from sweating.

Blacks have slightly more apocrines than whites, although

the reason is yet undetermined. Asians, in contrast, have a low distribution of apocrines. In fact underarm odor among Japanese is so rare that it is actually considered a sickness and at one time served as a legitimate excuse from entering into the Japanese armed forces. Due to an unusually low distribution of apocrines, Koreans are among the least odor-producing humans on earth, and 50 percent of them have no scent glands at all.

Coordination and Athletic Ability

Surveys of athletic abilities show that black children, on average, have a clear edge over whites or Asians in running and jumping activities. Muscular coordination develops earlier in black infants (a trait shared with aborigines) than in whites, although no one knows why. According to statistics, this edge apparently remains throughout adulthood: In 1989, blacks made up 12 percent of the U.S. population, yet 52 percent of NCAA basketball players that year were black. Nine out of the ten starters in the 1989 NBA All-Star Game were black as well.

Although some cite cultural differences for the unusually high representation of blacks in some sports, others feel that physical comparisons between whites and blacks suggest otherwise. Blacks from certain parts of Africa, for example, have significantly longer arms and legs and shorter torsos than whites on average. Researchers discovered in a study years ago that black Olympic sprinters averaged 86.2 centimeters in leg length, while their white rivals averaged 83. The athletes surveyed also had slightly less fat and slightly more muscle than their white counterparts.

More recent research shows that top black Olympic sprinters have more "fast-twitch" muscle fibers, which contract quickly and more powerfully than the "slow-twitch" fibers found in many whites. According to medical examinations, the muscles of 1988 Olympic champions Carl Lewis and Florence Griffith Joyner, for example, consist of more than 70 percent fast-twitch fibers.

Slow-twitch, or "endurance" fibers as they're known in running circles, are less explosive but work far longer before tiring out. Olympic marathon champion Joan Benoit Samuelson was found to have 79 percent slow-twitch muscle fibers.

Birth Defects
Extra fingers (six to a hand) occur seven times more often among black babies as among whites, whereas white babies have a higher incidence of harelip. Congenital dislocation of the hip is more prevalent in Japanese infants than in blacks or whites. Albinism occurs more often among American Indians than any other race.

Disease Prevalence
Some races are more vulnerable to certain diseases than others. Jews, for example, suffer the world's highest incidence of Tay-Sachs disease, a metabolism disorder, while the Irish suffer most from spina bifida, or cleft spine. Pima Indians of Arizona have a 50 percent incidence of diabetes among those 35 and older, a rate ten times higher than the rest of the U.S. population. Many blacks from West Africa evolved special sickle-shaped corpuscles in their blood to protect them from malaria, but the adaption is clearly a mixed blessing. These corpuscles can also block small blood vessels, causing oxygen deprivation and tissue destruction that can lead to death. Although many blacks are protected from malaria, about 80,000 of West Africans die each year from sickle-cell anemia, while only 9 percent of American blacks carry the sickling gene.

LANGUAGE DIFFERENCES BETWEEN RACES

Our three races speak over 4,000 languages and 20,000 dialects. Some, like Anus, Bella Coola, Blood, Bok, Gold, Grawadungalung, I, Kukukuku, Nupe, OK, Ron, Santa, Tiini, and

U, are spoken by as little as a few thousand people. Others, like Chinese Mandarin, will have nearly a billion speakers by the turn of the century. India boasts the greatest diversity, with 845 different languages spoken.

Language	Number of Speakers Worldwide (millions)
Chinese Mandarin	713
English	391
Russian	270
Spanish	251
Hindi (India)	245
Arabic	151
Bengali (India)	148
Portuguese (Portugal, Brazil)	148
German	119
Japanese	118
Malay-Indonesian	112
French	105
Urdu (Pakistan)	70
Punjabi (India)	64
Italian	61
Korean	59
Telegu (India)	59
Tamil (India)	58
Marathi (India)	56
Cantonese (China)	54
Bihari (India)	50
Ukrainian (USSR)	42
Vietnamese	40
Polish	39
Gujarati (India)	28

Alphabets

The Cambodian alphabet is longest with 72 letters. The Rotokas in the South Pacific island of Bougainville is the shortest with only 11 letters.

Chinese is one of the most difficult languages to write because of its use of characters instead of letters. The character "xie," for example, requires 64 pen strokes, and means "talkative." The character "yu" requires 32 strokes, and means "to urge or implore." Studies show that words are recognized faster by the brain when drawn out as characters rather than letters.

Most Unique Language

The most unique language is !XU, spoken by natives of southern Africa and made famous by the main character in *The Gods Must Be Crazy*. !XU consists of 95 different consonants, 48 of which are made by clicking the lips, tongue, and teeth.

"M" Is for Mother

In almost every language on earth, the word for *mother* begins with an "m" sound. This may be due to the fact that babies all over the world learn the consonant *m* first.

▼▼▼▼▼▼▼▼▼▼▼▼

Our
Genders

WHAT'S THE DIFFERENCE?

For centuries men have been viewed as the superior sex. After all, men are generally bigger and stronger and until recently have exclusively controlled everything from politics to heavy industry.

With an increasing number of women moving into positions of power, however, a different view of the sexes has begun to emerge. "Male-bashing"—the pointing out of men's many weaknesses—has become exceedingly common. Women's strengths, meanwhile, have been highlighted, toppling the age-old myth of male supremacy and in some cases casting the qualities of men as distinctly inferior.

When the data are carefully analyzed, however, it turns out that neither sex is superior but simply different, as can be evidenced in the following gender comparisons.

Smiling
Women smile more than men. One can find immediate proof of this by thumbing through any high-school yearbook.

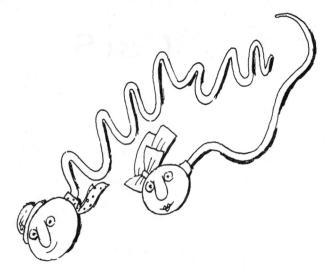

Last Out of the Starting Gate, First Across the Finish Line

While males generally outdistance females at the onset of life, they tend to fall behind rapidly after that. Male sperm (Y) typically swim faster than female sperm (X) and consequently have a better chance of reaching and fertilizing an egg. That's why 125 boys are conceived for every 100 girls. Female sperm are slower only because they carry a heavier load of genetic material, necessary to construct a body capable of pregnancy. Females, in fact, mature faster in the womb and are actually born with a four- to six-week headstart over males.

Health Factors

Males die sooner or more often in 57 of the 64 major causes of death. While women typically tolerate fatal infections longer than men, they nevertheless appear to suffer from a greater number of nonfatal illnesses. Lupus, an inflammatory disease related to arthritis, for example, strikes women 8 times as often as men, increasing to 15 times more frequently during childbearing years. Not only do women suffer 10 times more headaches than men but they are also more prone to acute respiratory and gastrointestinal problems, as well as arthritis, anemia, diabetes, hypertension, and some forms of heart disease. Women miss work slightly more often than men, but this is probably due to better overall health consciousness.

Physiological Differences

Physical Factor	Male	Female
Brain weight	49.4 ounces	45 ounces
Heart weight	10 ounces	8 ounces
Blood quantity	1.5 gallons	.875 gallons
Percentage of body weight:		
Water	60 percent	54 percent
Muscle	42 percent	36 percent
Fat	18 percent	28 percent
Bone	18 percent	18 percent
Lung capacity (at age 25)	6.8 quarts	4.4 quarts
Breaths per minute (at rest)	14–18	20–22

Longevity

After spontaneous abortions and stillbirths are taken into account, the male/female birth ratio drops from 105 to 100. During the first year of life, 54 males die for every 46 females. By age 21, there are 68 male deaths for every 32 female deaths. By age 65, finally, there are about 7 surviving men for every 10 women. Women outlive men in nearly every corner of the globe and specifically in the United States by more than 7 years.

As of 1985 women in the United States could expect to live seven years longer than American men. Some researchers claim women have stronger immune systems, a special adaption for the added physical stress of pregnancy, and are therefore better equipped to fight off disease. Consider, for example, the difference in the sex chromosome pattern: XX for females, XY for males. The XY pattern is known to predispose men to more diseases, such as hemophilia and some forms of muscular dystrophy. Other experts claim—as we previously noted—that women simply take better care of themselves and see their physicians more often. Still others cite the "height" factor— that is, tall people tend to die sooner than short people. It would follow then that men, being the taller sex, would die younger.

Recent studies indicate that there is at least some truth to each of these theories. However, none of them can explain why this age differential is largely a product of the twentieth century only. In 1900 the life spans of men and women were nearly the same, separated, in fact, by a mere two years.

Enter the new fashion of cigarette smoking. At the turn of the century men took up this pastime in droves. Women, however, continued to refrain from smoking, since it was considered unladylike. As the years progressed, the incidence of lung cancer and heart disease in men began to skyrocket. Indeed, twice as many men die today of lung cancer and heart disease as women.

If it weren't for the cigarette factor, men who are not killed by violence (accidents, homicides, wars, and so on) could expect to live just as long as women. After all, the world record for longevity, 120 years, is held by a man. According to a 1983 study, the life expectancy of men who smoke fewer than 20 packs of cigarettes in their lives are statistically equal to those of women when male deaths attributed to violence are removed.

Who Gets What?

Males Suffer More From:	Females Suffer More From:
Accidents	Anemia
Cancer*	Diabetes mellitus
Gastric ulcers	Femoral hernia
Gout	Gallstones
Heart disease*	Hypertension
Hepatitis	Lupus
Inguinal hernia	Migraine
Kidney stones	Myasthenia gravis
Leprosy	Obesity
Substance abuse	Osteoporosis
Tuberculosis	Rheumatoid arthritis

*Women are catching up to men in these categories, due to increased cigarette smoking.

Personality Disorders and Substance Abuse

Since men are commonly more aggressive (in part due to greater amounts of the male hormone testosterone), they're consequently more prone to accidents, violence, and stress-related illnesses.

Men cause two-thirds of road accidents, although women have been catching up in recent years. Males—particularly the young who have the highest testosterone levels—also commit far more homicides (14,629 compared to women's 2,085 in 1987) and assorted acts of violence (261,548 aggravated assaults compared to women's 40,186 in 1987). Contrary to popular belief, however, women commit more child abuse than men (48 percent to 42 percent according to one recent survey).

Men are particularly vulnerable to personality disorders, such as antisocial behavior, as well as drug and alcohol abuse. Women, on the other hand, suffer more from anxiety, phobias, and depression and are more likely to attempt suicide, although more men actually succeed at it.

Marriage increases the risk of depression for women and decreases the risk of depression for men.

Athletic Ability

Young adult males average 50 percent muscle and 16 percent fat. Females of the same age category have 10 percent less muscle and 10 percent more fat. Due to their larger hearts and lungs, males enjoy an 8 percent higher rate of aerobic power. Such attributes give men the edge in sports involving running, jumping, throwing, hitting, or lifting.

Women, however, have proven themselves equal to or better than men in long-distance swimming, precision archery, small-bore rifle shooting, and certain forms of gymnastics.

There is even evidence that women are closing the gap in those sports where men now excel. For example, in the 1968 Olympics, the 200-meter backstroke gap between men and women was 11.7 percent. In 1984, the gap was narrowed to 5.1 percent.

The Senses

Tests reveal that women possess slightly keener senses than men. Specifically, women display more accuracy at identifying odors and tastes; better perception of high sound frequencies (they're more easily awakened by an infant's cry, for instance); greater sensitivity to touch; and sharper vision with a far lower incidence of color blindness than men.

Learning

Women perform left-brain–oriented tasks better than men. Evident even in childhood, for example, girls generally boast a superior capacity for processing language: they speak their first words sooner and go on to show better verbal abilities throughout life. Boys are not only slower to speak but are also more apt to suffer from speech impediments and/or

42

learning disabilities, such as stuttering and dyslexia. Girls can also sing in tune earlier and keep a beat significantly better than boys can.

Men, on the other hand, excel at right-brain–oriented tasks. Baby boys gain mobility before baby girls and later outclass them in mathematics, science, and visual-spatial tasks.

Technological Innovation

Although women score higher on IQ tests, male preponderance in technological innovation is probably the most significant psychological difference between the sexes. In part due to cultural conditioning, only about 1,500 of the 70,000 patents granted per year in the United States go to women. As of 1988, women were receiving only 5 percent of the Ph.D.s in physics and 7 percent of those in engineering.

OUR SEXUALITY

Human beings are among the most highly sexed animal species on earth. Unlike many animal species, human females are ready for intercourse 365 days a year. And the act itself may be indulged in for a period of one hour, two hours, or even an entire evening.

Such activity eclipses that of our close relatives, the baboons, who take a mere 8 seconds with a total of 15 thrusts to complete intercourse. Lions may take even less time copulating.

The Mangaians of Polynesia are the most highly sexed people in the world: an 18-year-old Mangaian couple on average makes love three times a night, every night, and their sex life doesn't begin to decline until approximately the age of 28, when the frequency drops to twice per night.

The Peak Years

The potential for human sexual reproduction generally is not attained for females until the onset of menstruation, between the ages of 10 and 14. Males, as a rule, cannot experience ejaculation until the age of 11 or 12.

Males typically reach their physical peak during the late teens when the number of orgasms that can be achieved is at its highest and erections can be maintained for up to an hour. By age 70, erections last only seven minutes or less.

Females, on the other hand, don't reach their sexual peak until their early thirties, and more are able to achieve orgasms during this time period than at any other age.

From a reproductive perspective, the peak years for human sex are between the ages of 20 and 29. Maximum fertility for both males and females is reached at around age 24. When women reach their thirties, however, fertility declines rather sharply and the chances of bearing a child with some chromosomal abnormality is 5 for every 1,000 births. At age 40, the risk increases to 15 per 1,000 births; at age 45, the risk escalates considerably to 50 per 1,000 births.

In Broad Daylight

Contrary to popular belief, the best time for engaging a sex partner is not in the dark of night but instead during the day, when the sun shines brightest. Studies indicate that sun-

light arouses sex drive by stepping up the activity of the pituitary gland, which regulates the ovaries and testes.

Darkness, in contrast, signals the pineal gland in the brain to produce melatonin, a substance that inhibits ovulation, sperm production, and hormones responsible for sexual desire. Melatonin levels, in fact, are five times higher during the night. This may explain why blind people who perceive continuous darkness have lower fertility rates than normal.

The Season for Sex

Studies reveal that levels of testosterone—the hormone that regulates sex drive—are highest in men during the months of optimum sunlight in the summer and early fall and lowest in winter.

According to the Institute for Sex Research at Indiana University, the rate of intercourse peaks in the month of July, during the longest and sunniest days of the year. Statistics also show that fertility rates, contraceptive sales, and outbreaks of venereal disease all peak in summer and early fall. This may well be because, due to the rigors of winter, the young of most species are likeliest to survive if they are born in the spring. A high copulation rate during the previous summer and fall helps assure that more newborns will arrive in spring or early summer.

Sex by the Clock
The most universal time for sex in the United States is 11 P.M., especially on a weekend. According to a recent report in the *New England Journal of Medicine,* women are 30 percent more sexually active during a full moon.

Racing Heart
In the first stages of sexual arousal, pulse rate will rise from 70 to 80 per minute to 90 to 100. Moments before orgasm, it may climb as high as 130 and up to 150 during orgasm. Blood pressure may shoot up from 120 to 250 at climax.

The Look of Love

Humans may be said to become their most attractive during sex play. Pupils commonly dilate (the pleasure response), while the surface of the eyes takes on a glistening sheen. As excitement grows, blood is distributed from the interior of the body to skin surfaces. The lips become moist and full. The skin not only becomes hotter to the touch but also flushed, especially in women.

In 75 percent of women, the skin surfaces of the abdomen, breasts, and neck may actually take on the appearance of a rash, which vanishes soon after orgasm. Nipples become erect in both sexes, but this is most noticeable in women. Even the breasts themselves may be affected, increasing in size by as much as 25 percent during foreplay.

WHAT YOUR PARENTS NEVER TOLD YOU

Sexiest Parts of the Body

The sexiest aspect of a woman is her smile, according to the men surveyed by *Glamour* magazine. Women surveyed by the *London Sunday Times* found the sexiest part of a man to be his buttocks.

Orgasm and Ejaculation

Multiple orgasms are experienced by 14 percent of women, with second and third orgasms being the most intense. A woman's orgasm has more spasms and lasts 5 to 10 seconds longer than a man's orgasm. In some women, an orgasm may even last as long as a minute. In men, the first orgasm is always the strongest and lasts about 10 seconds.

Only 10 percent of women ejaculate during orgasm, and the composition of this ejaculatory fluid resembles the semen of men who have had vasectomies.

Wet Dreams

Studies indicate that 83 percent of young males experience "wet dreams," or nocturnal emissions, with the highest frequency—once per month or more—occurring in the teen years. Such wet dreams typically dissipate by age 30.

Heterosexual Fantasies

The most universal heterosexual fantasies, according to Masters and Johnson, are as follows:

Male
1. New or different partner
2. Being raped by a female
3. Observing another couple
4. Homosexual encounters
5. Group sex

Female
1. New or different partner
2. Being raped by a male
3. Encounters with females
4. Idyllic encounters with unknown men
5. Group sex

Positions

Due to better control of thrusting, the partner on top achieves orgasm more often than in any other position.

In recent surveys, at least 85 percent of heterosexual couples reported practicing oral sex during foreplay, nearly double the number of couples surveyed in the 1940s.

Alternative Partners

A Kinsey survey projects that by the age of 45, nearly 13 percent of females and 37 percent of males will have experienced some form of homosexual activity to the point of orgasm and that 3.6 percent of females and 8 percent of males will at some time participate in a sexual act with an animal.

Supersexy Women

As a general rule, women who produce the greatest quantity of the male hormone testosterone are the most sexually active and enjoy it more. Some women produce 10 times more testosterone than others. The highest levels of testosterone are produced during the middle of the menstrual cycle, when women are notably more responsive.

Masturbation

The universal practice of masturbation has even been observed in infants. Self-stimulation in the form of fondling may occur several times a day in some infants, who exhibit extreme annoyance if efforts are made to interrupt them, according to sex researchers.

The dog, cat, porcupine, elephant, and even the dolphin (by holding its penis in the jet of a water intake or rubbing it against the bottom of the tank) have also been observed in masturbatory acts.

Eighty percent of women and 94 percent of men masturbate, and surveys show that men masturbate about twice as often as women. Masturbation rates based on age, sex, and marital status are provided in the table below as originally compiled in a Masters and Johnson survey.

Males	Times per Year
Ages 16–20	57
Ages 21–25	42
Married	24

Females	Times per Year
Ages 18–24	37
Married	10

Multiple Partners

Before public awareness of the AIDS crisis, homosexual men were overwhelmingly the most promiscuous segment of American society, with 28 percent of men having reported over 1,000 different partners in their lifetimes. Today heterosexual men are thought to be the most promiscuous, with about 75 percent of all married men having engaged in at least one extramarital fling. According to recent surveys, the incidence of marital infidelity can be broken down as follows. For husbands:

Years Married	Percentage Reporting Extramarital Sex
0–2	15
2–10	23
10–20	30
20–50	75 (various statistics)

For wives:

Years Married	Percentage Reporting Extramarital Sex
0–2	13
2–10	22
10–20	22
20–50	50

Homosexuality

Relationships between members of the same sex are hardly a new phenomenon. In fact, marriage between two women or two men was legal and accepted in the early days of the Roman Empire. Several Roman emperors, including Nero, were married to men.

The most universal homosexual fantasies, according to Masters and Johnson, are as follows:

50

Male
1. Imagery of male sex anatomy
2. Being raped by a male
3. Heterosexual encounters with a female
4. Idyllic encounters with unknown men
5. Group sex

Female
1. Being raped by a woman
2. Idyllic encounters with established partner
3. Heterosexual encounters
4. Recalling past experiences
5. Sadomasochistic imagery

Pornography and Erotic Imagery

Studies indicate that sex crimes decrease when "nonviolent" (no bondage or other forms of sadomasochism) pornography is made available to the public. However, violent pornography depicting scenes of sadomasochism appears to have the opposite effect.

Rapists, child molesters, and other sex offenders surveyed said they had *less* exposure to pornography during adolescence than the average person.

In most surveys men say they are highly aroused by erotic imagery in films. Although women claim to be only slightly aroused, when checked in laboratory research for physiological response—heart rate, perspiration, and vaginal lubrication—they turn out to react as strongly to such imagery as men.

Sex in Retirement Years

While 70 percent of men are still sexually active at age 70, this figure drops to 50 percent at age 75. Women are slightly less active, due to a shortage of men.

The number one cause of impotence is circulatory problems, especially in older men. Hardening of the arteries, a result of a lifetime of high-cholesterol diet, occurs first and foremost in a man's penis, slowing blood flow and inhibiting erections.

Sex and Race

Surveys show that blacks engage in sex on a more frequent basis and have more orgasms than whites. They in turn have more foreplay and sex than Japanese couples whose children typically sleep with them until puberty.

The Penis

The average male penis when erect measures six inches in length. The majority of women surveyed say penis length is of little or no importance when it comes to sexual enjoyment.

By comparison, the African elephant's penis weighs 60 pounds. The blue whale's penis averages ten feet in length. Some species of lizards and snakes actually have two penises.

THE CHEMISTRY OF LOVE

Love Me, Love My Pituitary

The euphoric feeling of love is not a product of the heart; instead, it is rooted in neural pathways and hormones emanating from and regulated by the pituitary gland. When damage or alteration of this organ occurs, the hormones and nerve pathways controlling pair-bonding are cut off.

People who have had surgery for a pituitary tumor during their childhood or early teens, for instance, may never fall in love. "These people can show affection," a Johns Hopkins University love expert notes, "but most of them will never experience pair-bonding, the phenomenon most of us call falling in love."

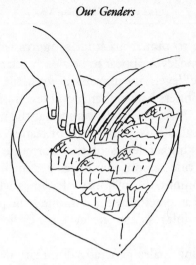

R_x *for a Broken Heart*

Chocolate contains phenylethylamine, the same chemical the brain produces when people fall in love. The chemical causes a happy, slightly dreamy feeling by stepping up heart rate and the body's energy levels. One study has shown that people frequently crave chocolate after breaking up with a lover.

Testosterone

The highest levels of testosterone, known primarily as a male hormone, are produced in men just after sunrise. Men might recognize this as the "morning rise," when erections seem to appear for no apparent reason.

All of the following activities or events cause testosterone levels to rise in men:

- Thinking about or actually engaging in sex
- Moderate exercise
- Fighting
- Watching violence on TV
- Success/winning a sporting event
- Intense emotional expression

According to numerous studies, aggressive behavior and high testosterone levels appear to be closely related. An analysis of testosterone levels in university wrestlers, for example, showed that winners had higher blood levels of the hormone than losers did. A similar study found that the most aggressive hockey players also have high levels of testosterone.

Men have higher levels of this hormone than women, which may be one reason why males get into more trouble. Young men commit the majority of crimes when their hormone levels are at a lifetime peak. Among male prison inmates, the higher the adult testosterone level, the earlier the age of the first arrest.

While young males generally dominate everything from business to conversations (in mixed groups men talk and even interrupt more than women), a curious reversal—likely related to shifts in testosterone production—occurs after middle age. During their fifties and sixties men gradually become quieter while women become more dominant and assertive. Testosterone declines in males at the rate of 1 percent per year until age 60 or so, when blood levels then drop to that of a nine-year-old boy. Meanwhile, the hormone increases in the female after menopause. In fact, some postmenopausal women actually sprout facial hair, and their voices may even deepen and become husky.

PART
2

OUR MINDS & SENSES

▼▼▼▼▼▼▼▼▼▼▼▼

Our
Brain

OUR MIRACULOUS MEMORY

Picture a hot dog smothered with mustard and relish and
steaming hot. Can you see it? Smell it? Taste it?

You can. Yet the hot dog doesn't even exist.

To create the hot dog, your brain fired off hundreds of
electrochemical impulses between its neurons (gray cells
topped with treelike branches). These impulses helped to open
a vast file cabinet of memories: hot dogs eaten at baseball
stadiums; hot dogs sizzling over grills; undercooked hot dogs;
burnt hot dogs; squishy hot dogs; in other words, a compila-
tion of every hot dog you've ever seen, sniffed, or tasted.

Although seemingly instantaneous, the act of calling up an
entire pushcart of hot dog experiences takes the brain a bit of
time. Thoughts and memories travel relatively slowly in the
brain, varying from 3 to 300 miles per hour. That's slower than
household electricity. A single hot dog memory uses just one-
tenth of the energy found in a single particle of visible light.
In fact, the total output of the brain is a mere 20 watts, not
even enough to power the average light bulb.

The memory is capable of retaining about 100 billion bits

of information, or 500 times the information contained in a complete set of encyclopedias. We can thank the brain's 100 billion neurons and 100 trillion connections for those memories—46 ounces of memories in all, if you're average.

The brain triples in size from birth to adulthood, but from adulthood to the retirement years it shrinks by more than an ounce. Between 30,000 and 50,000 brain cells die each day and, unlike other types of cells in the body, they are not regenerated. By around age 65, one-tenth of these cells are gone.

The ability to form memories peaks in the twenties and begins to decline gradually thereafter. Important data and memories, however, are "associated" in several locations throughout the brain, so few long-term memories may actually be lost. This helps to explain why older people often remember the distant past but frequently forget trivial short-term data, such as what they ate for breakfast.

When Is Memory Best?

The average person can remember a five- to seven-digit telephone number when viewed briefly one time. For five seconds look at the number below.

614920813106053815

How well you recall the numbers may depend on what time of day you look at them. Short-term memory has been found to be 15 percent more efficient in the morning and long-term memory more accurate in the afternoon.

New Tasks, Repetition, and Memory

If one finger is numbed for a prolonged period, its corresponding brain area will shrink. But if a finger is used in a new way—for instance, when learning to play the piano for the first time—or is used more than normal, the corresponding area in the brain will actually grow as it learns. In general, repetition strengthens the connections between brain neurons, thus improving memory.

Photographic Memories

Eidetic, or photographic, memory is extremely rare and is usually only seen in young children. In most cases this extraordinarily vivid recall disappears with the acquisition of language, although the reason is yet unknown. The great English historian Thomas Macaulay was said to possess such a memory. He reportedly wrote histories without referring to reference books and could repeat a chapter of a book verbatim after reading it only once. In order to win a bet, Macaulay actually memorized *Paradise Lost* in a single night.

The world record for an eidetic memory feat is held by Bhandanta Vicitasara of Rangoon, Burma, who in May of 1974 recited from memory 16,000 pages of Buddhist canonical texts.

INTELLIGENCE FACTORS

Test Testing

Ninety-five percent of the U.S. population scores between 70 and 130 on IQ tests. The highest recorded test score belongs to Marilyn Jarvik of St. Louis, Missouri, whose IQ at ten years of age measured 228. The number of people with an IQ this high is estimated to be less than one in a million.

The brains of people who perform well on IQ tests actually spend less energy than poor performers and are thought to have more efficient neural circuitry. Interestingly, blood flow to the brain while thinking is greater in women than in men, which may be part of the reason women score the highest on IQ tests.

Einstein's Brain

The brain maintains a superior performance level by keeping itself "clean"—that is, when neurons in the brain die of disease, injury, or even old age, they are quickly consumed and digested by neuroglial cells that provide nutrition to healthy neurons.

A researcher at the University of California found that a specimen of Albert Einstein's brain had 73 percent more neuroglial cells than average, a possible link to his genius.

Idiot Savants

Science has documented a number of people with low IQs who are nevertheless gifted in a particular area, such as art, music, or mathematical calculation. Mentally retarded or autistic people with such "islands" of talent are known as idiot savants.

The idiot savant syndrome is caused by damage to the left hemisphere of the brain before, during, or after birth. The left hemisphere develops in the fetus later than the right and suffers a greater risk from prenatal influences. To compensate for the damage, the right hemisphere enlarges, becomes dominant, and in some cases "overdevelops." The result in extreme cases is a savant with superhuman right-brain skills.

The ratio of male to female idiot savants is 5 to 1. This disparity is thought to be caused by male fetus production of the masculinizing hormone testosterone, which can impair brain development in rare instances. Female fetuses are protected because most of the circulating maternal testosterone is safely taken up by the placenta.

Some famous idiot savants:

■ Born three months premature, autistic identical twins George and Charles were kept in incubators for 60 days. In early adulthood, within seconds they could calculate the day of the week on which a date fell over 40,000 years ago and could also describe weather conditions on any randomly chosen day of their lives. And although the twins could repeat 300 digits in order from memory, neither was able to add, subtract, multiply, divide, or count higher than 30.

When separated from each other a few years ago, their astonishing skills diminished.

■ In 1920 at the age of 38, "K" had a mental age of 11, with a vocabulary consisting of only 58 words. Amazingly, however, he could remember the population of every U.S. town and city over 5,000, as well as the distances of each city from New York or Chicago, the county seats in all U.S. counties and the names, room numbers, and locations of 2,000 U.S. hotels. By its population number alone, "K" was able to recognize any city in the United States.

■ In the 1700s, Jedediah Buxton was known as a "lightning calculator." With a mental age of 10, he thrilled neighbors, friends, doctors, and journalists with his lightning calculations of mathematical problems. When asked how many cubic 1/8ths of an inch exist in a body whose three sides are 23,145,789 yards, 5,642,732 yards, and 54,965 yards, he answered with the correct 28-digit figure.

■ Alonzo Clemens, brain-injured from a fall at age three, has an estimated IQ of 40. Yet Alonzo sculpts animals with remarkable precision. He can create a horse or a bull or a dog from a lump of clay with the finest detail of muscle, tendon, and fiber in just twenty minutes. His pieces today sell for $350 to $3,000, with some commanding prices as high as $45,000.

■ Blind and mentally retarded Leslie Lemke has astonished audiences nationwide with his extraordinary piano-playing abilities. He can play back any piece of music flawlessly, no matter how complex, after hearing it only once. On one occasion Leslie played back 45 minutes of music he had just heard for the first time and accurately recalled every note.

TWO BRAINS IN ONE

The brain is divided into two equal halves, or hemispheres. The right half controls the left side of the body, while the left half controls the right. The two brains are virtual mirror images of each other, yet their functions differ remarkably. To illustrate the various functions of the two brains, consider the abilities that may be lost when either hemisphere is damaged through injury or disease.

Left-Brain Damage

Language and speech deficiencies. Stroke victims often lose their speech when the brain's left hemisphere is cut off from its normal flow of blood. If the egg-shaped patch—known as Broca's area—in the left frontal cortex is injured, coordination of the muscles of the face, tongue, jaw, and throat becomes impossible. Injury to Wernicke's area, located next to the auditory cortex, causes a patient to speak an odd gibberish, where inflection, rhythm, and grammar are correct but the words are meaningless. A typical patient with Wernicke's aphasia may utter a statement like "Yes, the fribble nosis on wubbtes, but I mebciz grobble on the frizzes tables."

Although a left-brain–damaged victim is often unable to speak, he may be perfectly capable of singing, since the right hemisphere of the brain controls this ability.

Word deafness. When the connections between the auditory cortex and Wernicke's area are injured, word deafness occurs. Victims can read, write, and speak normally but are unable to comprehend the spoken words.

Name amnesia. Left-brain damage often impedes the ability to recall names of familiar people. Interestingly, the right brain is largely responsible for recognizing faces, but it is the left brain that stores names. This is why even "normal" brains have a tough time connecting names to faces.

Right-Brain Damage

Loss of depth perception, spatial orientation, and other visualization processes.   People with right-brain injuries frequently find it difficult or impossible to assemble simple jigsaw puzzles or follow directions on a map. They sometimes become disoriented in familiar buildings and may even get lost in their own homes.

Loss of perception of the left side of the world.   The right brain processes images from the left eye. Victims who suffer the bizarre disorder, known as "neglect," ignore or fail to perceive objects on the left side of their bodies. Some brain-damaged patients shave only the right side of their face or ignore food on the left side of a dinner plate. When asked to draw a clock, they may only draw the right-hand side. One victim of this disorder refused to acknowledge the existence of his left arm that had been paralyzed.

Amusia.   Musicians with amusia literally forget how to play their instruments and may even lose the ability to sing.

Inability to express emotion.   A small area in the right frontal cortex of the brain is responsible for vocal nuances and gesturing. When this area is damaged, people lose vocal inflection and may sound flat or "dead," even when attempting to express joy.

Many emotional states are associated with the cerebral cortex, and particularly with the right hemisphere of the brain. Right-brain–damaged patients are frequently unconcerned with their disabilities because the vital emotional processing centers responsible for worry and depression have been impaired. Consequently, the left-brain–damaged patient is usually the one most devastated with feelings of loss and depression over his injuries or disease.

Prosopagnosia.   The inability to identify faces, including those of close family members, is a hallmark of this disorder. In severe cases, victims may not even recognize themselves in a mirror. However, a prosopagnosia patient will frequently recognize a friend's face as soon as he hears the person speak, as the left side of the brain is responsible for voice recognition.

ON THE OTHER HAND: HAND-BRAIN CONNECTION

Why We Are Left-Handed

Some studies indicate that babies who usually lie with their heads to the right become right-handed; those who turn to the left become left-handed. Most cases of left-handedness, however, are thought to be caused by minor brain damage before or during birth. Many scientists believe the damage is due to reduced oxygen supply before birth.

The evidence, however, relies heavily on statistics. Twins, for example, have a high proportion of neurological problems due to crowding in the womb and are twice as likely to be left-handed as singletons. The mentally retarded, epileptics, and children with learning disorders are also disproportionately left-handed. The largest population of lefties is found among autistics: 65 percent favor their left hand over their right.

On the other hand, some of the world's greatest geniuses, including Leonardo da Vinci, Michelangelo, and Benjamin Franklin were southpaws. The incidence of left-handedness is higher than average among the world's artists.

Southpaw Astronauts
Though 1 out of every 10 people on earth is left-handed, the incidence of lefties in NASA's Apollo Space Program was found to be 1 in 4.

Health and Lefties
Migraines, allergies, dyslexia, stuttering, skeletal malformations, and thyroid disorders are all suffered more by lefties.

Lefties, however, recover better from strokes than righties because 40 percent of them use *both* sides of the brain to process speech, instead of the left side only, as righties do.

65

THE BRAIN'S "PHARMACY"

The brain acts as its own pharmacy, producing more than fifty psychoactive drugs that affect memory, intelligence, sedation, and aggression.

Endorphin, for example, is the brain's version of the pain-killer morphine, but it is three times more powerful. These natural painkillers are frequently released during physical exertion, such as long-distance running and laughter. (This may be why laughing makes us feel so good.)

Serotonin, on the other hand, is known for its mood-altering effects. Diminished levels of serotonin in the brain have been linked to both depression and aggressive behavior. In one study, arsonists and murderers were found to have significantly smaller amounts of serotonin in their brains than normal. Another study suggests that eating carbohydrate-rich foods triggers the production of serotonin and that some people crave such foods when levels of this chemical are low in the brain. Doctors are currently experimenting with serotoninlike compounds to treat depression.

Dopamine, meanwhile, has been found to make people more talkative and excitable. Researchers at Stanford University discovered that many shy people have a lower concentration of this brain hormone than gregarious people. A group of prescription drugs called monoamine oxidase inhibitors increase levels of dopamine in the brain and are being used by Columbia University scientists to successfully treat timidity in some people.

Hunger is regulated primarily by cholesystokinen, another brain hormone. Laboratory mice with a deficiency of cholesystokinen have insatiable appetites and literally eat everything in sight, including their cages. In humans, the hormone may some day be used to help correct eating disorders or to aid in dieting.

Coffee is known to improve test scores. According to numerous studies, caffeine stimulates the cerebral cortex and spinal cord, improving concentration and memory as well as speeding up reaction time.

The Hungry Brain

The more than 100,000 chemical reactions that occur in the brain each second require huge amounts of the body's stored energy. In fact, the brain can burn as many calories in intense concentration as the muscles do during exercise. That's why thinking can feel as exhausting as a physical workout.

A deficiency of iron causes the brain to get less oxygen than normal, decreasing attention span and concentration and increasing irritability. The brain also absorbs more harmful metals, such as cadmium (from drinking water through galvanized pipes and from cigarette smoke) and lead (from car exhaust fumes and industrial pollution), when the body's iron levels are low. Both metals are associated with poor mental performance.

Exercise, on the other hand, increases the amount of oxygen reaching the brain by as much as 30 percent, thus boosting mental efficiency.

BRAIN BUSTERS

Seeing Sounds, Hearing Colors

One of the most astonishing brain disorders is a phenomenon known as *synesthesia,* in which the body's senses are somehow confused and overlapped. According to neurologists, some people with this disorder can actually *see* sounds, *taste* words, and *feel* flavors. In one case a woman in Oklahoma saw the sound of a kitten purring as a long chain in the air. A ringing telephone made diamond-shaped blocks in the air. Another woman with synesthesia actually tasted words: *Republican,* for example, tastes like peach cobbler, and *New York* tastes like toast. One man claimed to feel flavors: sour tastes felt pointy, and chicken felt angular.

The most common form of synesthesia is "audition colorée," when the sight of colors creates sounds in the listener's ears. When a researcher monitored the brains of test subjects as they experienced these "colored" sounds, he found that blood flow decreased in the neocortex and increased in the limbic system. During the process of colored hearing the brain's higher information processing apparently turns off, and an older, more primitive way of seeing the world takes over. Little more is known about this disorder except that similar hallucinations can be brought on by LSD.

The "Unfeeling" Brain

Because it has no nerve endings, the brain can be burned, frozen, hit, or cut without the slightest sensation. This explains the reason neurosurgeons in many cases are able to operate on patients without anesthetizing them. (Headache pain is caused by blood vessels that lie over and outside the brain.) However, a surgeon who touches specific parts of the brain can make other body parts respond. A probe in one spot, for instance, starts the hand tingling; touching another spot triggers a tingling response in the foot, and so on. Even memories can be probed in this manner. By electrically stimulating the temporal lobe, vivid memories of long forgotten sights, sounds, and smells can be brought back to life.

Brain Death

The brain continues sending out electrical wave signals as long as 37 hours after death.

Our
Inner Clock

THE TIME OF OUR LIVES: OUR INNER CLOCKS

Most people can wake up in time for work in the morning without the use of an alarm clock, according to researchers at Duke University. Studies prove what many of us have suspected all along: we all have our own internal clocks. What's more, these clocks can be trained for accuracy.

Groups of people were tested at Duke University to see if they could wake up within ten minutes of a specified time. All sounds were removed from the sleepers' rooms, so only an internal cue could be utilized for arousal at the proper time. A high percentage of the subjects were able to wake themselves, regardless of the designated awakening time. This innate ability, researchers believe, is tied to the normal cycles that occur during sleep.

Birth and Death

Other internal clocks dictate when mothers will give birth. Oddly enough, most normal births occur between 12:00 A.M. and 8:00 A.M., much to the inconvenience of the expectant couple.

71

The majority of deaths also occur in the early morning hours. In fact, if you're still alive at ten in the morning, chances are good that you'll live to see another day, no matter how sick you may be.

Circadian Rhythms

Circadian rhythms are the approximate 24-hour cycles by which most of our body functions are regulated. Throughout the day, over 100 internal functions—such as cell division, adrenal gland activity, DNA synthesis, body temperature, blood pressure, and hormone production—peak at various times. Energy levels, sensory alertness, and moods are all affected by these natural oscillations. We may feel terrific at ten in the morning and simply rotten three hours later. The body isn't playing tricks; it's just making necessary adjustments.

Like a supersophisticated thermostat, a small cluster of cells in the hypothalamus gland schedule the body's adjustments to be in rhythm with the environment. The rising and setting of the sun, the waning and waxing of the moon, and even seasonal changes play an important role in how these cells govern and "set" the body's internal clocks.

HOW THE BODY CHANGES THROUGHOUT THE DAY

7 to 9 A.M.

The body is gearing up for the day ahead. Heart rate increases, body temperature rises, adrenal hormones peak. Result? More people over 65 suffer heart failure and stroke now than at any other time of day. The majority of all deaths, including suicides, occur at this time.

Asthma sufferers, however, receive the maximum benefit from their medicine soon after waking, and the least in the afternoon and evening.

9 to 11 A.M.

Following the worst portion of the day is one of the best. Clinical tests show that after 9 A.M., the body is least sensitive to pain and anxiety levels are lowest. Psychiatrists believe this is a good time to make important decisions because one is apt to be more rational.

Alertness peaks in late morning when body temperature is high. Short-term memory is 15 percent more efficient now, and problem-solving abilities are also sharper than average.

Noon

Eyesight is sharpest at midday.

1 to 2 P.M.

Energy levels and alertness drop temporarily. Scientists speculate that such early afternoon blahs may be an evolutionary adaptation to limit activity when the sun reaches its highest point in the sky and the body is most prone to heatstroke and sunburn. Animals frequently take shelter at this time, particularly in equatorial regions.

3 to 4 P.M.

The best time for athletics: muscle strength, body flexibility, and aerobic capacity are at their peak. Long-term memory is significantly better at these hours. A second peak in death rate, however, occurs at 4:00 P.M. Statistics show an unusually high number of traffic fatalities at this time.

5 P.M.

Blood pressure peaks. Taste and smell are sharpest, which probably reflects the body's anticipation of the largest meal of the day. Incidentally, most family fights occur just before supper.

6 to 7 P.M.

This is the worst time of day to eat a large meal if you're dieting. More calories end up as fat now than in the morning, due to fluctuations of the body's metabolism.

8 to 11 P.M.

In order for the body to rest and restore itself, the brain hormones serotonin and adenosine shut down the electrical activity of some neurons, causing drowsiness and sleep. As our body temperature drops, our metabolism slows down. Hearing, however, remains acute throughout the night, an evolutionary adaptation to help alert us to danger during this most vulnerable time period.

Midnight to 3 A.M.

Blood pressure, heart rate, and stress hormones all bottom out during these hours. Contrary to folklore, the least number of deaths in any 24-hour period occurs after 11 P.M. Heart attacks rarely strike at midnight because the body is in its most relaxed state. But expectant couples beware. The most common time for the onset of labor in pregnant women is 1 A.M.

4 A.M.

Even in a well-heated room, one is likely to feel chilly because body temperature now drops to its lowest level of the day.

Workers unaccustomed to a midnight shift are most likely to feel drowsy now, causing job performance to plummet. Statistics show that industrial accidents are unusually high at this hour. The nuclear accident at Three Mile Island took place at 4 A.M. and was blamed on "human error." And a warning to asthmatics: the body steps up its production of histamine now, increasing wheezing attacks.

MONDAY MORNING BLUES

Sleeping late on weekends will make our Monday morning blues even bluer, according to researchers at the Stanford Sleep Disorders Clinic. The reason is simple: most people "run" on an overstressed biological clock.

While most of us are geared for an 11 P.M. to 7 A.M. sleep schedule during weeknights, we "reset" our internal rhythms on weekends. On Fridays, we may stay up until midnight, waking at 8 A.M. On Saturdays, we may slip even farther away from our weeknight schedule, turning in at 2 A.M. and waking at 10 A.M. When Sunday night rolls around, weekend partners may try to resume their regular 11 P.M. bedtime schedule but instead find themselves the victims of insomnia. Although we may realize that it's foolish to go to bed three hours early—at 8 P.M.—in the middle of the week, we don't realize that the same standards also apply to Sunday nights. If we're lying in bed when our internal clock is telling us we should be awake, it's not surprising that the mind is very active, thinking about work we may have to face the next day.

And the Monday morning blues? If we've pushed our weekend schedule hard enough, rising at 7 A.M. on Monday morning is the equivalent of 4 A.M. body time, the sleepiest part of the internal cycle.

Our
Sleep &
Dreams

THE PURPOSE OF SLEEP

Although the mechanics of sleep are slowly revealing themselves to scientists, the question "*Why* do we sleep?" remains an
enigma.

One theory maintains that sleep evolved as a way of protecting animals during nighttime, the most dangerous period
of the 24-hour cycle. When animals are snoozing quietly in a
burrow or up in a tree, for example, they're far less likely to be
discovered and eaten by a predator.

Another theory hypothesizes sleep as a means of conserv-
ing calories. Running about 24 hours a day burns huge
amounts of energy, making it necessary for an animal to hunt
down more food, which may be scarce to begin with, thus
increasing the chances of death through starvation. Sleep im-
mobilizes the body, allowing fewer calories to be burned and
thus less food to be required for survival.

Finally, some scientists believe the function of sleep may
be related to a combination of all these factors.

Although the purpose of sleep remains hypothetical, we
nevertheless possess a body of validated information on *how* we

77

fall asleep, the mechanics of brain activity *during* sleep stages, and the content and implication of *dreams*. Let's examine these in turn.

FALLING ASLEEP

Pandiculating

For most humans the first step in falling asleep is pandiculating. How many times have you pandiculated today? If you were bored, anxious, or just plain tired, you probably pandiculated several times—particularly if you saw other people doing so. *Pandiculating* is the medical term for yawning, a bodily function largely shrouded in mystery.

No one is really sure why we yawn. For years it was believed to aid us by drawing in more oxygen to the lungs. But the new school of thought holds that yawning may actually provide too much oxygen for the lungs to process. A yawn is usually followed by a brief period of apnea—that is, a cessation of breathing.

Today doctors believe that feeling of rejuvenation we get after a good yawn comes not from increased oxygen intake but from the expulsion of excess carbon dioxide in the blood. Such a hearty yawn results in improved circulation, which occurs when the muscles of the neck and chest stretch and contract.

Psychotics rarely yawn, and people who are severely ill tend to refrain from yawning until their condition improves. Physicians often recognize a yawn as one of the first signs of recovery.

All animals yawn, even fish and reptiles. Baboons yawn to intimidate rivals by exposing their canines.

Presleep Hallucinations

The "fall into sleep" begins with a series of quick visual images—a phantom slide show, known as *hypnagogic hallucinations.* These presleep visions are usually only mundane snapshots of events experienced during the day, but they can startle us awake on occasion if they become too realistic. Most often these hallucinations lure us gently into sleep, but not into the dream-state, and are thus quite different from actual dreams.

Spiraling into Sleep

Teetering on the edge of sleep, we may begin to experience a floating or falling sensation, a universal phenomena that most people find quite pleasant. The eyes begin to move with slow, rolling motions as if watching a huge ball rolling over and over. We are now "spiraling" into the abyss of sleep.

The Presleep Spasm

Sleep actually begins with a quick, reflexive twitch of the legs, arms, or head, clinically termed a *myoclonic jerk.* This body spasm, which usually goes unnoticed but can potentially bring us to full wakefulness, is caused by a sudden explosion of electrical brain activity and is similar to an epileptic seizure. After the myoclonic jerk, sleep begins instantly.

THE STAGES OF SLEEP

Once asleep, we go through four distinct stages. The first stage of sleep is marked by an easing of muscle tension and a change in brain-wave activity. This transitional stage is especially light and typically lasts about 20 minutes, during which time you may be easily awakened.

In stage two, brain waves slow and slumber grows deeper. Even with eyes taped open, we are quite literally blind during this phase and would be incapable of seeing anything—even a hand passing over the face—since the eye-brain connection has been shut off. More than half of the time devoted solely to sleep is spent in stage two and no dreaming occurs.

Stages three and four are marked by even slower brain waves, but the deepest sleep occurs in stage four. Mysteriously, the highest levels of the body's growth hormone are released during this sleep stage.

After cycling back for a few minutes of stage-two sleep, dreaming begins.

THE MYSTERIOUS WORLD
OF DREAMS

Our Dream Patterns

Dreams originate in the right hemisphere of the brain, and each of us—that is, with the exception of those who suffer right-brain damage—dreams whether we remember doing so or not. As a general rule, we must wake up during dream sleep in order to remember our dreams. Because they spend 25 percent more time dreaming than adults, children therefore remember their visions more often.

Sleep researchers have found that everyone experiences changes in sleeping position just before and just after the dream phase as a necessary adjustment to help recirculate the blood.

Once in the dream-state, motor neurons responsible for muscle contraction are chemically inhibited. Except for the eyes, the mouth, and the fingers and toes, all major body parts become immobilized. This is a necessary function to keep us from getting out of bed and acting out our dreams. In some people, however, the sleep-paralysis mechanism is dysfunctional and sleepwalking occurs, with results ranging from the humorous to the fatal.

As dreams occur, the eyes may move rapidly back and forth as if watching actual movement. This is known as rapid-eye-movement (REM) sleep. Body reactions during REM sleep are amazingly similar to those produced by a mild panic attack: heartbeat and breathing speed up; more sweat and stomach acid is produced; and blood pressure and cholesterol levels increase. Most REM sleep is decidedly sexual as well. While dreaming, the penis and clitoris engorge with blood, causing them to stiffen.

This first dream phase, lasting only a few minutes, is the shortest of the night. When dreaming is over, the sleeper retraces all the stages back to lighter sleep and then repeats the deep-sleep stages back to dreaming again.

Dream duration increases as the sleeper continues to move into each successive sleep cycle. The final dream period, just before morning, may last for over an hour and most frequently involve dreams about our past.

Emotional content also intensifies the longer we dream. The most bizarre dream scenarios—flying, nudity, and Shakespeare-quoting crocodiles, for example—almost invariably arrive toward morning.

Infants and Dreaming

Infants dream more than adults. Those born prematurely dream even more, and fetuses dream nearly all the time. The nature of their dreams, of course, is a mystery.

Dreams of the Blind

People who have been blind since birth dream of sound and textures and can sometimes be seen "feeling" imaginary objects in their sleep.

Sleep Talking

Talking out loud during dreams is common in children as well as adults: approximately 70 percent of people commonly babble in their sleep. The talk, however, is frequently fragmented and usually makes sense only to the sleeper.

The Dreaming Heart

Some people's hearts stop beating when they dream. This cessation may last for as briefly as a few seconds or as long as nine seconds.

Most Common Dreams

According to surveys, the five most universal dreams, in order of frequency, are:

1. Falling
2. Being pursued or attacked
3. Trying to perform a task but repeatedly failing
4. Work and school activities
5. Sexual experiences

People between the ages of 18 and 28 are more apt to dream of strangers than any other age group. Older people dream more of family members. Parents dream more of their children, and children dream more of their parents. Until the last decade or so, women dreamed most of familiar, indoor settings, but with more women moving into the work force the "home setting" dream is being replaced by career and outdoor scenarios. Men dream twice as much about men as they do women. Men also dream more about jobs, adventure, and sports, and their dreams center on more aggressive themes— sometimes incidents of violence with strange males or sex with unknown women.

The most frequent dreams of children feature their parents and friends, and of being frightened by wild animals or insects. Dreams of animals steadily decline as children age.

Pregnancy and Dreams

In the first six months of pregnancy women dream most about their husbands; in the last three months they dream more about babies. These baby dreams are sometimes unnervingly vivid. Expectant mothers sometimes dream that the baby has already been born and is walking or even talking. Nightmares feature infants that are born too big or too small. On occasion, some women dream of giving birth to animals or a half-dozen babies at one time. Such dreams may be brought on by daytime anxieties and hormonal changes due to the pregnancy.

A study conducted by San Francisco's Neonatal and Obstetrical Research Laboratory revealed the following most frequent dream topics of pregnant women, classified by stage of pregnancy:

1st trimester: frogs, worms, potted plants
2nd trimester: cute, furry animals (such as kittens)
3rd trimester: lions, monkeys, Barbie dolls

Nightmares

Generally speaking, the more stress we face during the day, the more likely we'll suffer from bad dreams at night. The most common causes of nightmares are anxiety, depression, exhaustion, and tranquilizers.

Death Dreams: A Warning?

Dreams of death or separation from loved ones are often meaningless but can potentially signal that a serious illness—such as heart disease—may be worsening, according to research at the University of Rochester Medical Center. A study of 49 patients revealed that seriously ill men and women who dreamed of death or separation tended to get sicker.

Such death dreams seem to indicate that the unconscious mind actually senses when an illness is becoming more severe and attempts to communicate what it knows through dream imaging.

The onset of many diseases can actually be predicted by sleep anomalies; for example, some older people who sleep more than 10½ hours or less than 4½ hours per night may be heading for a serious illness. Studies show that cancer, heart disease, and other major illnesses are usually preceded by unusual sleep durations. The key word here, of course, is *unusual:* a sudden *change* in sleeping habits, not *how much* a person sleeps, should raise a warning flag.

OTHER SLEEP TRIVIA

Sleep Duration Over a Lifetime

Age (years)	Daily Sleep Duration (hours)
Fetus	Nearly continuous sleep
Newborn	19
6	11
12	8
25	7½–8
40	7
48	6
60	5½

85

Some studies suggest that people need less sleep as they age. Furthermore, sleep disturbances from physical ailments, such as apnea, increase as we get older.

Sleeplessness

Sleep deprivation lasting more than 48 hours typically causes hallucinations and psychosis. The world record for going without sleep is 11 days (264 hours and 12 minutes), a feat considered extremely dangerous by sleep researchers.

30 million Americans suffer from sleep disorders. Most men begin having problems falling asleep in their mid-twenties; women have the same difficulty during their mid-forties.

While normal sleepers change body positions about 30 times per night, insomniacs may toss and turn more than 100 times.

Missing Your Partner

Sleep studies show that if your sleeping partner is absent in your sleep, you'll almost always move over to the side of the bed normally occupied by him or her.

Napping

An afternoon nap is healthy. One study indicates that afternoon nappers are 30 percent less likely to suffer coronary artery disease, although the reasons behind this are not yet known.

Animal Snooze

Humans stay awake far longer than many animals. Bats, cats, porcupines, lions, gorillas, and opossums sleep 18 to 20 hours a day, and some woodchucks snooze for as long as 22 hours. Pigeons frequently open their eyes during sleep to watch for predators. The dolphin, remarkably, only "half" sleeps: its brain shuts down only one hemisphere at a time.

Dream sleep has been observed in all animals studied except the spiny anteater. Horses and rats dream 20 percent of the time during sleep. Cows kept in barns dream 40 minutes per night, while cows sleeping in meadows dream only half as much.

The Creativity Link

Studies show that creative people, problem solvers, and neurotics sleep longer, have more dream sleep, and wake up less refreshed than other people. Albert Einstein reportedly slept ten hours per night. On the other hand, Napoleon, Winston Churchill, and Thomas Edison all reported sleeping six hours per night or less.

When Most Americans Wake

Time (A.M.)	Percentage of People Out of Bed
Before 6	25
Between 6 and 7	32
Between 7 and 8	14
Between 8 and 9	5
After 9	5

(Night workers account for the other 19 percent.)

Our
Ears &
Hearing

HOW HEARING WORKS

You know the sound of a cat when you hear it. You know, too, a cat's mood simply by tuning in to its voice patterns. A *purrrr* means contentment. A *pthththt!* means rage or sudden fear. And who doesn't recognize the familiar howl of a cat who has just had its tail stepped on? Cats are indeed fortunate that our

human brains can differentiate between an "I'm feeling mellow" meow and a "Get off my tail!" meow.

Although you can't "see" a meow, its sound makes distinct wave patterns as it travels through the air. Different sounds make different patterns.

The sound waves that enter the ears are bounced off the eardrums, which resonate in response. Depending on pitch and volume, the eardrums may vibrate slow, fast, soft, or hard.

Three tiny bones in the middle ear—the hammer, the anvil, and the stirrup—receive the vibrations, amplify them, and send them on to the snail-shaped cochlea with its 25,000 tiny hair cells. The cochlea converts the vibrations into electrical signals, which are transmitted to the auditory nerve, and then to the auditory cortex on each side of the brain. The brain instantly sifts through its file of cat memories, pulls out a memory that matches its needs, and orders the body to respond with appropriate action—in this case, taking out the can opener and opening a snack for kitty.

Ear Sensitivity

For detecting some sound frequencies near 3,000 hertz (vibrations per second), the vibrations of the eardrums may be as small as 1 billionth of a centimeter, or 1/10th the diameter of a hydrogen atom!

Humans can hear frequencies as high as 20,000 hertz (higher than the sound of a piccolo) and as low as 20 hertz (lower than a bass fiddle).

Human versus Animal Hearing

Vampire and fruit bats can hear pitch as high as 210,000 hertz, ten times higher than humans. The dolphin's hearing is even more sensitive, with an acuity of 280,000 hertz. Both the bat and the dolphin use high-frequency hearing in sonar detection.

The best overall long-distance hearing, on the other hand, belongs to the fennec, a small African fox. Its oversized ears enable it to hear the movements of another animal up to one mile away.

Sound Location: Why We Have Two Ears

Depending on its origination, sound usually reaches one ear a fraction of a second faster than the other ear. By calculating the difference in receival times between ears, the brain can pinpoint a sound source within two or three degrees.

The owl is even more accurate at placing sounds because one of its ears sets slightly farther forward than the other. Such an adaption allows the owl to locate a sound within one degree.

Why We Can't Hear Internal Body Functions

Evolution has provided us with ears that can detect high-pitched sounds better than low ones. That's why we can hear a woman's voice from farther away than a man's: Specifically, under typical conditions the male voice can be discerned from about 200 yards away; the female voice, slightly farther. If our ears were tuned to sounds any lower than this, we would be able to hear the gurgles and swooshes of our own body func-

tions, including the sound of blood coursing through our arteries. In fact, in the part of the ear where vibrations are converted to nerve impulses, there are no blood vessels at all because our own pulse would be deafening. Instead of receiving blood, this area is constantly bathed with dissolved nutrients.

Our Voice on a Tape Recorder
When we speak, the sound of our voices is conducted by our bones, which slightly alter timbre. This explains why many people are often unable to recognize the sound of their own voice when played back on a tape recorder, because only "air-conducted" sound is recorded. Like the tape recorder, friends hear our voices through air conduction alone.

Our Musical Ear
Scientists have found that within the "nonmusical" population as a whole the left ear is better at recognizing melodies than the right ear; however, the right ear of trained musicians is superior.

Stop the Music!
The African Bushman lives in a quiet environment and has no measurable hearing loss at age 60. By comparison, 60 percent of American college students already suffer from some high-frequency hearing loss, according to a study by the University of Tennessee's Noise Laboratory. The cause of this premature "deafness" is noise.

Hearing loss has long been linked to exposure to noise. Sustained loud noise—from jet aircraft, trucks, motorcycles, stereos, food processors, and so on—actually destroys the tiny hair cells of the ear's cochlea. These hair cells are a vital component of the auditory system and the more that are destroyed over time, the greater the hearing loss. The ability to hear high-pitched sounds, which declines in acuity in Americans from infancy on, is affected first. Even fetuses are at risk. According to a Japanese study, a fetus exposed to a noisy environment develops more slowly in the womb and weighs less than normal at birth.

According to the Environmental Protection Agency (EPA), one out of every two Americans is regularly exposed to harmful noise levels. The EPA defines the cutoff point for danger with the following guideline: "Any time you have to raise your voice to be heard, the background noise is too loud and should be avoided."

Sound, measured in decibels, can reach extremely dangerous levels as illustrated below.

Levels resulting in instant and irreversible hearing loss:

Activity/Distance	Decibel Level
NASA rocket taking off/ 100 feet	190

Levels resulting in permanent damage after consistent exposure:

Activity/Distance	Decibel Level
Jet taking off/100 feet	130–140
Drum set/3 feet	120–130
Loud rock concert/ front row	110–120
Car horn/20 feet	110

Levels resulting in damage after daily exposure of 8 hours or more:

Activity/Distance	Decibel Level
Food blender/2 feet	100
Chainsaw/jackhammer/ 2 feet	100
Heavy truck/10 feet	90
Lathe machine/1-2 feet	90
Inside moving car	80
Inside noisy office	80

Safe levels after daily exposure:

Activity/Distance	Decibel Level
Normal conversation	50–60
Quiet library	30
Whisper/5 feet	20

The Future of Ear Wiggling

The ability to wiggle the ears is a vestige of evolution, a throwback to a time when our ancestors could "cock," or adjust, the ears to aid in hearing. The musculature for ear cocking has gradually diminished over the eons through genetic reprogramming. Most of us have lost the ability to move the ears at all in such a manner. But like most vestigial elements, the musculature will probably remain within some family lines for thousands of generations to come.

Our
Nose &
Sense of Smell

WHAT THE NOSE KNOWS

The nose is directly connected to the brain's limbic system, which plays a vital role in evoking and regulating emotions. When we smell a rose, we do more than smell. In fact, we may suddenly recall a romantic evening with a lost love.

Odor molecules are all around us. Sniff deeply and they rush up into the nostrils where they're warmed and humidified to prepare them for identification. Contrary to popular belief, the nostrils do not do the actual smelling. The epithelium, a pair of mucus-coated patches of cilia located behind the bridge of the nose just below the brain, reach out and snare incoming molecules, which, like puzzle pieces, are locked into corresponding receptors at the ends of tiny olfactory nerves located within the epithelial membrane. The nerves signal the olfactory bulbs, which in turn relay electrical impulses to the smell cortex and to other interpreting brain centers. Depending on the scent signals received, the brain may react with joy, repulsion, fear, or even a sense of nostalgia. Some scents stimulate the hypothalamus and pituitary glands to release hormones controlling sex, appetite, and body temperature.

OTHER NOSY NEWS

Nasal Defense System

The nose's relentless flow of mucus is the first line of defense against the billions of airborne bacteria that are constantly trying to invade the body. Strong chemicals in mucus dissolve many of these disease-causing organisms. Those that manage to survive are swept to the back of the throat and eventually swallowed. Acid in the stomach usually finishes them off.

Larger or more irritating particles, such as pollen grains, face a different defense system. These more offensive invaders stimulate the trigeminal nerves, which react with a prickly sensation, triggering a sneeze that can eject particles at speeds exceeding 100 miles per hour.

Sometimes the trigeminal nerves are short-circuited and sneezing seizures result. The world record for chronic sneezing is held by Donna Griffiths of Pershore, England, who sneezed continuously from January 13, 1981, to September 16, 1983, a total of 977 days.

The Off-Duty Nostril

Nostrils switch on and off every three to four hours, so that one is always smelling and breathing while the other closes down and rests.

The Compass in Your Nose

All humans have a trace amount of iron in their noses, a rudimentary compass found in the ethmoid bone (between the eyes) to help in directional finding relative to the earth's magnetic field.

Studies show that many people have the ability to use these magnetic deposits to orient themselves—even when blindfolded and removed from such external clues as sunlight—to within a few degrees of the North Pole, exactly as a compass does.

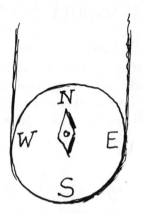

A researcher from England's Manchester University found that when a magnet is placed on the right side of the head, the directional accuracy of test subjects falls 90 degrees to the right. When a magnet is placed on the left side, the error falls 90 degrees to the left, proving conclusively that humans are profoundly affected by magnetic fields.

Though no one knows how this "sixth" sense is processed by the brain, more than two dozen animals, including the dolphin, tuna, salmon, salamander, pigeon, and honeybee, have been found to have similar magnetic deposits in their brains to help them in navigation and migration.

Nature's Most Awesome Sniff Detectives

The bloodhound's epithelial membrane, or "sniffing organism," is fifty times larger and thousands of times more sensitive than a human's. The trace of sweat that seeps through your shoes and is left in your footprints, for example, is a million times more powerful than the bloodhound needs to track you down.

But even a hound's nose is outsniffed when measured against the silkworm moth. A male can detect and follow 1/10,000th of a milligram of the female's sexual attractant up to seven miles away.

SCENT AND SENSIBILITY

I Remember It Smell

The notion that odor memories are more powerful than visual ones is nothing new. Tests show, in fact, that visual memories decline by 50 percent after 3 months while memories associated with smell decline by only 20 percent, even after a full year.

Women Have More Sensitive Noses

Women have a better sense of smell than men due to higher levels of the female hormone estrogen, known to activate the olfactory receptors.

Interestingly, a woman can detect the odor of musk—a scent associated with male bodies—better than any other odor. When estrogen levels peak during ovulation, a woman's smell is most acute and can detect musk 100 to 100,000 times more keenly than during menstruation.

Sex-Scent Connection

The sex/scent connection is a powerful one. About 25 percent of people with smell disorders—due to either head injuries, viral infections, allergies, or aging—lose interest in sex. A growing body of research indicates that pheromones, a subtle body odor that attracts and excites sex partners in animals, are also produced in the apocrine glands of humans. When exposed to female pheromones, men experience faster beard growth. Exposed to male pheromones, women become more fertile and have less irregular menstrual cycles and milder menopause symptoms.

Women are affected by the pheromones of other women as well. When women live together for any length of time, their menstrual cycles automatically become synchronized.

Calming Scents

Scientists at Yale University have found that some fragrances have a calming effect on humans and can actually lower blood pressure. Yale has even taken out a patent on apple-spice fragrance because of its uncanny ability to stop panic attacks in some people.

The smell of a beach has the same relaxing effect, according to a study at England's University of Warwick. Researchers found that anxiety levels decreased as much as 17 percent after subjects smelled a "beach perfume" containing essence of seaweed.

The Lifesaving Odor

The human nose is extremely sensitive to the smell of rancid meat. We can detect 1/400-billionth of a gram of this rotting essence—chemically known as methyl mercaptan—in a quart of air. Identifying decaying flesh was probably vital to our ancestors' survival in the wild, and it continues to save lives today. Methyl mercaptan is the chemical that we smell in leaking gas—put in as an additive by utility companies for quick detection.

Detecting Disease by Smell

Many diseases give off a telltale odor all their own. Some physicians can detect these diseases simply by sniffing their patients. In emergency rooms, for example, physicians must sometimes diagnose the cause of a coma by smelling the coma victim's breath: a sweet smell, like acetone, may indicate diabetes; an ammonialike odor points to some malfunction of the kidneys; and the smell of excrement often indicates a bowel obstruction.

Some genetic diseases have even been named for their odors. Osthaus disease, a genetic disorder, has a very distinct aroma. A scientist at Washington University School of Medicine describes an osthaus as a place where malt is cured before beer is made. People afflicted by this disease have an odor distinctly like malt. He also cites further examples, such as maple-syrup urine disease, in which accumulation of certain acids causes the urine to have a caramel-like smell, and a rare condition called "sweaty feet disease," which is caused by a defect in fat metabolism. Infants with this disease smell like a locker room.

Infection by *Pseudomonas* bacteria smells distinctly like a musty wine cellar, while arsenic poisoning smells like garlic.

Other diseases with distinctive odors are included in the following list:

Disease	Odor
Some cancer types	Fetid
Diphtheria	Sickeningly sweet
Eczema and impetigo	Moldy
Measles	Freshly plucked feathers
Plague	Apples
Scurvy	Putrid
Smallpox	Putrid
Typhoid fever	Freshly baked bread
Yellow fever	"Butcher shop" odor

Addison's Disease

Addison's disease, a malfunction in the adrenal glands, can make a person abnormally sensitive to odors. Victims of Addison's disease (President John F. Kennedy was among them) are sometimes able to detect odors 100,000 times more acutely than normal.

Phantom Odors

In addition to auditory hallucinations, some schizophrenics may suffer from phantosmia, or odor hallucinations. Powerful enough to cause vomiting and fainting, these phantom odors are frequently so unpleasant and acute that patients may stuff their noses with cotton in a desperate attempt to block them out.

Our
Eyes &
Sight

THE EYES HAVE IT

Even after decades of study, human vision remains largely an overwhelming technical mystery.

To transmit this page of print to your brain, light waves must pass through the cornea at the front of the eye to the fluid-filled outer chamber, the aqueous humor, and then through the pupil, which dilates or constricts depending on the brightness of the light source. The light waves then continue on to the lens, which bends or thickens to keep the image in focus, through a second and much larger chamber filled with the jellylike protein vitreous humor, and finally to the retina at the back of the eyeball.

The retina is composed of rods and cones, two types of nerve cells that react to light. The rods, numbering 125 million, are concentrated around the sides of the retina and are responsible for processing black and white vision at night. The 7 million cones, on the other hand, lie mainly in the center of the retina and control the detection of color.

How the Eye Hoodwinks Us

Through a little-understood process of image-enhancement, the brain adds or fabricates fine details the eyes have missed. The final processed image, in fact, is a subtle composite of what the brain imagines it sees and what the eye actually sees. A good example of the brain "fabricating" images is a writer's supposedly "finished" manuscript. After careful checking, the writer insists that his work is free of spelling errors. The proofreader, meanwhile, locates dozens. The writer isn't lying about the misspellings; he's simply too familiar with the work to "see" past his brain's unconscious corrections. Such an example serves to illustrate why it is often not so much what the eye perceives as what the brain adds that is important.

Here is an example of the brain fabricating perceptual information by referring to its memories of logical angles and lines and confusing what the eye actually sees. The two horizontal lines are equal in length.

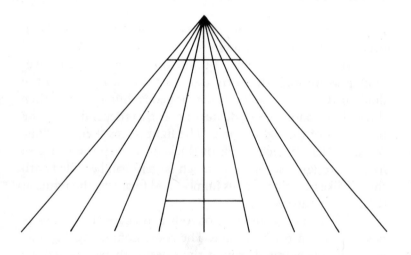

The Pupil

The size of the pupil in the center of the eye is controlled by the sphincter and dilator muscles of the iris, the colored part that surrounds the pupil. When light is dim, these muscles open the aperture of the pupil to allow the greatest amount of light to reach the retina. In bright light, the aperture is pulled smaller to avoid "blinding" the retina.

I Only Have Eyes for You

Pupils respond to emotion in a similar fashion. Anxiety, fear, and excitement enlarge the pupils, a reaction thought to be dictated by the brain's need to see more of what's happening in potentially dangerous situations. Unpleasant scenes not associated with fear, on the other hand, cause the pupils to constrict.

Pupil reaction, in general, is believed to reflect the level of interest or fascination in the mind of the viewer. Most men's pupils grow as much as 30 percent larger when viewing pictures of sharks and nude women but shrink considerably in response to pictures of nude men and infants. Women's pupils, in contrast, constrict when shown pictures of sharks and nude women but grow large when viewing nude men and infants.

Embryo Eyes

Before a human embryo turns one month old, eyes begin to form and measure about one inch long. At two months the eyes can be seen on either side of the embryo's head and then gradually migrate to the front of the face as the embryo grows.

Skew-eyed Infants

Many infants have the ability to move their eyes independently of each another, much to the surprise of their parents, but this talent is fleeting; in most cases the eyes begin working in unison after only a few months.

Muscle Workout

Eye muscles get the greatest day-to-day workout, moving some 100,000 times in any 24-hour period. To give the legs the same degree of exercise, 50 miles of walking would be required.

One Blue, One Brown

Helerochromia iridis, the one blue eye/one brown eye phenomenon, occurs in 2 out of every 1,000 people.

Eye Color and Dexterity

Studies show that people with dark eyes have faster reaction times than people with light eyes, and the same principle holds true for dark- and light-eyed animals.

While brown-eyed people perform better overall in sports that require split-second timing, blue-eyed people appear to excel in self-paced activities, such as golf and pitching. Evidence conclusively proves that brown-eyed baseball players make better batters, while those with blue eyes excel as pitchers.

Eye Dominance and Athletic Ability

As with right- and left-handedness, most humans favor one eye over the other and the one used most often determines who strikes out in baseball.

In a study of baseball players at the University of Florida, "cross-dominant" batters—that is, those who could effectively use either their right eyes and left hands, or their right hands and left eyes—hit significantly better than those who used the same eye and hand. Of the pitchers studied, however, the cross-dominant trait proved disastrous: they gave up many more runs than their uncrossed-dominant peers.

The best batters were those who used both eyes equally. Such "cycloptic" or balanced vision is genetically predetermined and occurs in only 17 percent of the population.

Eyes That Glow in the Dark

The glow emitted from the eyes of many animals in the dark is caused by light reflecting off the tapetum, a special retinal layer. The human eye lacks tapetum and thus absorbs all the light entering it.

Marigold in the Eye

In 1979, an eight-year-old boy in Cape Town, South Africa, was found to have a seed and a sprout growing out of his left eye. Botanists who examined the seedling discovered that the sprout was well on its way to becoming a marigold. The seedling was removed surgically, and the boy's eye healed.

Apparently the eye provides all the essential conditions for the germination of seeds: moisture, warmth, fresh air, and protection from strong sunlight.

Tears

With every blink, the eyes are bathed with a bacteria-fighting fluid secreted by the lacrimal glands in the lining of the eyelids. Additional fluid is released to wash out contaminants when the eyes become irritated.

Tears caused by irritants differ chemically from tears caused by sadness. Emotional tears contain 24 percent more of the protein-based hormones released by the body in response to stress: these include prolactin, adrenocorticotropic hormone, and leucine enkephalin, a natural painkiller.

Tear researchers believe the discovery in tears of prolactin, the hormone that stimulates milk production in breasts, may explain why women cry more often than men. Postmenopausal women cry less when their prolactin levels are lower.

Crocodile Tears

People with "crocodile-tear syndrome" shed tears when they salivate. Usually the result of an injury, this disorder is caused by a crossing of the nerves leading to and from the

salivary and lacrimal glands. Those afflicted literally cry in anticipation of food.

Color After Death
The eyes change color after death, most often to a greenish-brown.

VISIONARY MATTERS

Carrots and Night Vision
Carrots really do help sharpen vision. Vitamin A found in carrots is necessary for the proper functioning of the eye's rods, which promote adequate night vision. A healthy rod can be triggered by as little as one particle, or photon, of light. On a dark, clear night, the human eye can detect the light from a candle over 25 miles away.

The Eye's Blind Spot
The eyes of every human are afflicted with blind spots. There are no photoreceptors on the retina, where the optic nerve passes through; thus the eye is literally blind to any images that fall there.

Hold this book at arm's length, close your left eye, and focus on the dark circle in the box below. Keeping your left eye closed, slowly bring the book closer to your face. Between 10 to 14 inches from your nose, the X in the box should disappear. This is your blind spot.

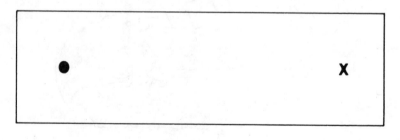

Seeing Specks

By staring into a bright blue sky it's frequently possible to "see" not only the outlines of blood vessels in your own eyes but also the floating blood cells and the seams in the lens membrane itself. Many people by their late twenties complain of seeing blurry black specks passing through their field of vision, which may be attributable to these visions of their very own eyes.

Old Lenses

The lenses of the eyes continue to grow throughout adulthood. Older people have the largest lenses, which are less pliable and less capable of focusing on nearby objects.

Color Blindness

Among Caucasian men, 8 percent are color-blind, compared to 5 percent of Asians, 1 percent of Eskimos, and ½ percent of women overall.

Color blindness is caused by either a defect in or the complete absence of the gene responsible for encoding one of the three pigments found in the retina's cones. The most common form of color blindness is the inability to distinguish red from green, while the rarest is "blue blindness."

Most animals are color-blind, or at least partially so. The giraffe, for example, sees some color but confuses green, orange, and yellow.

Noise, Tight Collars, and Vision

Because of their effect on blood pressure, both sustained loud noise and compression around the neck from tight collars or ties cause a temporary drop in visual acuity.

OUR BODIES

▼▼▼▼▼▼▼▼▼▼▼▼

Our
Skin

WHAT WE'RE WORTH

Not long ago, the human body's value was estimated at $1.98 on the basis of its chemical makeup. But times have changed. With the increased demand for organ and tissue transplants, the typical human body is now worth $200,000, according to the *New York Times.* Remember that when your banker asks for your net worth!

Component	Total Body Weight (%)
Water	61.8
Protein	16.6
Fat	14.9
Nitrogen	3.3
Calcium	1.81
Phosphorous	1.19
Potassium	0.24
Sodium	0.17
Magnesium	0.041
Iron	0.0075
Zinc	0.0028
Copper	0.00014
Other	0.2

THE NEED FOR TOUCH

A one-inch-long human embryo will pull its head back when its lips are lightly stimulated, proving the presence of the sense of touch as early as eight weeks. This is long before the embryo can either see or hear, testifying to the importance of this ancient sense.

Humans can survive without vision, hearing, or smell, but not without touch. Pain reception is necessary to warn the brain of hazards, such as fire or sharp objects. People afflicted with cutaneous alagia have dysfunctional pain receptors and often sustain life-threatening burns or other injuries because they cannot feel pain.

Studies show that even pleasurable touch is a biological need in many species. For example, newborn animals who receive stimulation of the skin through maternal licking grow up with a greater resistance to disease and are more likely to survive through adulthood than unstimulated animals. (Lambs may actually die at birth if their mothers neglect to lick and nuzzle them. According to breeders, Chihuahua pups have a notoriously high mortality rate because their mothers frequently are unwilling to lick them.) Stimulated animals gain more weight and are more active and less fearful throughout life as well.

A similar phenomenon has been noted in humans. Numerous studies indicate that infants deprived of fondling, holding, and caressing invariably suffer from depression, weight loss, disturbed sleep, a suppressed immune system and, in extreme cases, death.

Conversely, experts maintain that a frequently touched infant is often a healthy infant. Touch transmits a vital sense of security to the newborn by relieving stress and thereby boosting the immune system. Touch stimulation also benefits the circulatory process by improving blood flow.

Blind Touch

Many blind people have greater sensitivity in the skin than sighted people.

Sound Waves and Touch

Sound waves affect the sense of touch: low frequency sound desensitizes the skin, while high frequency sound makes the skin more sensitive.

A MIRACLE OF ENGINEERING

The skin is a miracle of evolutionary engineering: it waterproofs the body, blocks out and destroys harmful bacteria, regulates temperature, and continuously communicates with the brain. Functioning as the body's "feeler," the skin signals the brain to what is cold and what is hot, what is pleasurable and what is not. It can sense an object as tiny as 1/100th of a millimeter and can tickle us with goosebumps, irritate us with an itch, or startle us with pain.

Measured as a whole, the skin is the largest of all human organs: it weighs about six pounds on the average adult body and covers an area of 20 square feet on an adult male.

In only one square inch of human skin there are 19 million cells, 625 sweat glands, 90 oil glands, 65 hairs, 19 feet of blood vessels, 19,000 sensory cells, and over 20 million microscopic animals.

Bugs on the Skin

Every human's skin is infested with mites, even on the facial area. Impossible to wash off, they are thought to be beneficial by cleansing the follicles and unclogging glands. Although mites are transparent, you can see them with a strong

magnifying glass if you scrape your eyebrows with an index card and place the card in a dish with a few drops of water.

THE MEDICAL TEAM IN OUR SKIN

The skin serves as its own doctor. When flesh is cut, the skin teams up with the blood to mend the damage. While the blood forms a clot to seal the wound, special glands in the skin secrete an antiseptic to kill germs.

Blood vessels in the skin will shrink instantly in anticipation of an impending cut. You can observe the reaction by running the edge of a ruler over your forearm. The white line that appears is caused by a sudden loss of blood volume to help limit bleeding. After a moment—when your skin/brain connection senses that the danger has passed—the vessels will once again fill with blood and the line will turn red.

Bruises

A bruise is caused by burst blood capillaries near the surface of the skin. The "spilled" blood cells quickly die, change color, and are eventually carried off by the body.

The Skin's Thermostat

When the interior of the body grows too hot, blood vessels in the skin widen and take up more blood to help divert heat outwardly; as a result, the skin flushes red. When the body needs to conserve heat, on the other hand, the skin takes up less blood and turns pale.

Gallons of Sweat

The purpose of sweat is to help keep the body cool through evaporation. There are approximately 3 million sweat glands throughout the body. On an average summer day, these glands will pump out about two quarts of fluid composed of ammonia and salts. In a hot, desert climate these glands may produce as much as 2½ gallons of perspiration.

On humid days, sweat may fail to evaporate; instead, it may simply drip off the body with little or no cooling effect.

As a result, human survival time in very moist or humid air is much less than in dry air. In fact, when the surrounding air is completely dry, humans can survive a temperature of 266° F for up to 20 minutes. In moist air, 115 to 120° F is the maximum we can tolerate.

Goosebumps

The goosebumps that break out on our skin when we're cold represent little more than the body's effort to erect the coat of fur our ancestors lost over 100,000 years ago. Raised body hair provides added insulation.

Skin Color and Tanning

Prolonged exposure to the sun causes the skin to secrete melanin, a brown pigment that helps to block out harmful ultraviolet rays and promotes tanning.

Pregnancy hormones are similar to those which signal the skin to produce melanin. This explains why pregnant women tan easier and more deeply than others.

116

ONLY SKIN DEEP

Sags, Lines, and Wrinkles

Collagen—the skin's network of protein fibers—break down and become less pliable with age, causing sags, lines, and wrinkles to form on the face, neck, and hands. Any expression that manipulates the skin deeply and consistently will promote wrinkling (it takes about 200,000 frowns to create one permanent brow line), but exposure to sunlight and cigarette smoke hastens the process.

Acne

Acne is caused by overactive oil glands that are stimulated by hormonal changes in the body. The glands secrete too much oil and clog the skin's pores, causing inflammation.

Blackheads are masses of dead skin cells colored by the pigment melanin.

Dead Skin and Where It Goes

The body constantly sheds dead skin cells and replaces them with new ones. Thousands of these cells are lost, for example, every time we shake hands or swing a baseball bat. By the time we reach age 70, we'll have shed 40 pounds of dead skin.

Of the dust floating around in the average house, 75 percent is made up of dead skin cells.

Pain, Itch, and Tickle

Sensations sent from the skin travel at varying speeds, at times relaying information to the brain as fast as 230 feet per second.

Specialized sensory receptors located throughout the skin are responsible for signaling pain, with "prickling" pain traveling at 98 feet per second and "burning" pain at 6 feet per second.

Free nerve endings signal the sensations of itching and tickling, but at slower speeds.

Messner's corpuscle is the touch sensor largely responsible for the pleasant sensations obtained from a stroke or gentle caress. These sensors are spread throughout the body but are highly concentrated in the fingertips, lips, nipples, clitoris, and penis.

Nails

Fingernails, fine-tuned over the ages from claws, have a number of important roles—from protecting the fingertips from damaging blows to scratching an itch. They're also perfect for digging into tough-skinned foods, an adaptation that helped our ancestors survive in the wild.

Nails are made from hardened dead skin cells called keratin. Only the root, the part that can't be seen, is alive. From cuticle to tip, it takes the root about 150 days to push out a full-length nail, a growth rate of about 1/25th of an inch per week.

Possibly due to their greater exposure to sunlight, fingernails grow fastest in the summer and faster than toenails overall.

In right-handed people, the middle fingernail of the right hand grows fastest; in left-handed people, the opposite holds true.

The longest nails on record belong to Shridhar Chillal of Poona, India. Since he last cut them in 1952, the nails on his left hand have grown an average of 32 inches.

Our
Hair

HAIR GROWTH

Our primate ancestors were protected from the cold by a thick coating of hair all over the body. In our warmer world, all that remains of this magnificent coat is the small patch on the top of our heads and on the face of most men.

Hair is not alive, nor does it grow. The hair above the skin is actually dead protein that has been pushed through the scalp by hair follicles. These hair follicles, however, are very much alive, and about 5 million of them can be found throughout the human body. Only about 120,000 of these reside on the scalp. This relatively small number of follicles will produce as much as 100 feet of protein a day: that's seven miles of hair produced in a year, or 350 miles in the average lifetime. (By comparison, the Merino sheep produces 5,500 miles of wool fiber in a single year!)

Hibernating Hair

Hair grows in cycles. On the scalp, each hair grows continuously for 3 to 5 years and then enters a resting phase. After a period of 3 months or so, the hair is shed but not immediately replaced. Only after another resting phase of 3 to 4 months does the follicle grow a new hair. Ninety percent of the scalp is always in the growing phase.

Eyebrows and Eyelashes

Eyebrow hairs stay short because their growing phase only lasts for 10 weeks.

Eyelashes are replaced every 3 months. A person will grow about 600 complete eyelashes in a lifetime.

Beards

Beards grow more rapidly than any other hair on the body, and blond beards grow fastest of all. The average beard grows about 5½ inches in a year, or about 30 feet in a lifetime.

The longest beard on record was grown by Hans Langseth of Kensett, Iowa. At the time of his death in 1927 his beard measured 17½ feet.

Underarm and Pubic Hair

The purpose of underarm and pubic hair is to trap scent secreted by the apocrine glands, located in these areas in high concentration. The apocrine glands respond to emotion and become highly active when a person is sexually stimulated. Scientists speculate that scent collected in hair once helped our ancestors to attract and excite sex partners and may continue to play a similar—although highly diminished—role today.

Curly or Straight?

The amount of curliness in hair depends on the shape of the hair shafts. Straight hair is produced by circular shafts, wavy hair from oval-shaped shafts, and curly hair from kidney-shaped ones.

HAIR TODAY, GONE TOMORROW

Baldness

Male pattern baldness is responsible for the greatest amount of hair lost in men. One out of every five men begin balding rapidly in their 20s. Another one out of five will always keep their hair. The others will slowly bald over time.

As a general rule, the more hair a man has on his chest at age 30 the less hair he'll have on his head at age 40. The hormones (androgens) that produce chest hair are also responsible for male pattern balding, and the higher the hormone levels the greater the hair loss.

Women typically lose as much as 50 percent of their hair within 3 months of childbirth. This partial and temporary balding is caused by severe fluctuations of hormones.

Hair Growth and Loss

The average hair grows half an inch per month, with the fastest growth generally occurring in the morning hours. Hair sprouts fastest of all when you're in love, which may also be due to fluctuations of hormones.

A loss of about 70 hairs per day is typical, but emotional stress (including falling out of love), illness, malnourishment, and anemia can more than double this amount.

OTHER HAIR-Y ITEMS

Hair Color

Hair gets its color from melanocytes, special cells that deposit pigment in the roots. Melanin produces brown-black hair; phaeomelanin produces red, auburn, or gold hair. Graying is caused by a reduction of pigment, while a total absence of pigment produces white hair.

More redheads are born in Scotland than in any other country: 11 percent of its population has red hair.

Blonds and Lefties

According to a survey of 1,000 men and women at Beth Israel Hospital in Boston, natural blonds are twice as likely to be left-handed as brunettes and redheads.

Chemotherapy

Cancer patients treated with chemotherapy often lose their hair completely. When it grows back, it is frequently a different color than its original shade.

Raising Your "Hackles"

As a reaction to fear or cold, tiny muscles in the skin, called "erector pili," contract to force body hairs to stand on end. This reaction—most noticeable in dogs and cats—serves a dual purpose: it can make the animal appear larger and more ferocious and help prevent heat loss by lifting the skin around the shafts and closing the pores.

The Seminaked Ape

Although humans have as many hair follicles as gorillas, the "nature" of the hair differs. Gorillas are covered with larger "terminal" hairs, while humans are mostly covered with vellus, a fine, downy hair.

A Strange Case of "Thumb" Hair

During World War II, a wounded soldier received a skin graft to his thumb from a portion of his scalp. Hair flourished on the thumb and grew just as it would on the head. Years later, however, the thumb began to bald—ironically, at the same time as the soldier's scalp.

Our
Bones &
Muscles

BONING UP ON BONES

Bones provide the scaffolding necessary to hold up the body and to protect vital organs. The inside of bones, the marrow, produces blood cells; the outside of bones store and release calcium to aid in nerve conduction, muscle contraction (including heartbeat), and blood clotting.

Forty-five percent of bone is made up of mineral deposits, particularly calcium phosphate. Another 30 percent is living tissue, cells, and blood vessels. The remaining 25 percent is water. When their mineral content is removed, bones are supple enough to be tied into knots.

One of the strongest building materials known to man, bone can withstand stresses of 24,000 pounds per square inch, or about 4 times that of steel or reinforced concrete.

The Lonely Bone

The hyoid bone located above the larynx is used to anchor the muscles of the tongue and is the only bone that does not touch another bone. Because it is often broken when a person is hanged or choked, the hyoid is frequently used as evidence in strangulation homicides.

The Funny Bone

The ticklish pain we feel when hitting a certain spot in the elbow is not caused by the "funny bone," but by the ulnar nerve, located along the (aptly named) "humerus" bone. A blow compresses the nerve against a knobby part of the humerus, sometimes causing brief paralysis of the region.

Bones and Gravity

Bones must be exercised regularly to maintain their thickness and strength. Astronauts in zero gravity lose massive amounts of bone calcium after only a few weeks if they neglect to exercise. Even prolonged bed rest in normal gravity can cause bone deterioration. Marathon runners, by contrast, have among the thickest and strongest leg bones.

Feeling It in Their Bones

Rheumatoid arthritis sufferers generally feel increased pain in their joints about 12 hours before a rain. One study shows that many arthritics can detect even a slight difference in barometric pressure (as small as 7 millibars) simply by the difference in pain levels.

Calcium-Deficient Bones

When supplies of calcium in the bloodstream are too low, the body draws on the calcium reserves of the bones, eventually causing them to thin or even break. Such bone thinning, or osteoporosis, is a common problem among elderly women, who suffer more bone fractures than any other age group.

The Longest Bone

The longest bone on record was that of an eight-foot German, who died in 1902 in Belgium. His thighbone, or femur, measured 29.9 inches in length. The average femur, by comparison, is only 18 inches.

Sea Bones

The mineral content, porosity, and general makeup of human bone is nearly identical to some species of South Pacific coral. They are so alike, in fact, that plastic surgeons are using the coral to replace lost human bone in facial reconstructions. Instead of rejecting the coral—a problem with most transplants—the body's natural bone tissue infiltrates the coral and actually makes it stronger.

HOW BONES ARE DISTRIBUTED

Adult bones are distributed as follows:

Area of Bone Distribution	Number of Bones
Skull	22
Ears	6
Vertebrae	26
Sternum	3
Throat	1
Pectoral girdle	4
Arms and hands	60
Hips	2
Legs and feet	58
Ribs	24

There is one strange exception to this bone distribution: 1 out of every 20 people has an extra rib, and it is most commonly found in men. According to the Smithsonian Institute, 16 percent of Eskimo men and 7 percent of the Japanese carry a "spare" rib.

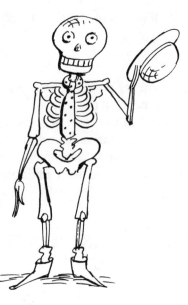

Male and Female

Scientists use several landmarks to distinguish a male skeleton from a female. A female has a wider and shorter breastbone, slimmer wrists, and a smaller and smoother jaw and skull; the male skull has a more slanted forehead and heavier brow ridges. Though the male skeleton is generally larger, a female has a wider pelvis, with a large, round birth opening in the center. The male's pelvic opening is smaller and more heart-shaped.

The Skeleton in Your Closet

Bone tissue is constantly being destroyed and replaced. About every seven years the body grows the equivalent of an entirely new skeleton.

The Incredible Shrinking Skeleton

Infants are born with 350 bones, many of which fuse during growth, so upon reaching adulthood the number of individual bones drops to only 206. Last to fuse is the collar-bone, and this occurs between the ages of 18 and 25.

The High Price of Bones

Human skeletons are in short supply. In 1989 the price of a skeleton made from real bones was $1,995. The plastic version, however, was only $380.

HOW MUSCLES WORK

The 656 muscles throughout the body are divided into two groups: the first, the voluntary muscles, are attached to the skeleton by tendons and aid the body in conscious movement; the second, the involuntary muscles, line the internal organs and contract automatically to regulate the heart, lungs, intestines, blood vessels, and glands.

Nerves running through the muscles receive electrical impulses from the brain, stimulating the muscles to contract. The muscles always work by shortening, or pulling, but never by pushing (even when you're doing push-ups). The range of body motion is possible through muscle "teams"—that is, every set of muscles has an opposing set of muscles to reverse motion.

Muscle is made up of tiny individual fibers and only rarely are all the fibers used in one muscle at the same time. Lift a light object, such as a book, and only a few fibers in the arm are used. Lift a heavier object, such as a television, and more fibers come into play. Each fiber contracts several times per second and must switch on and off thousands of times when sustained muscle power is needed.

Muscles fatigue when they run low on oxygen and nutrients. Heart rate and breathing speed up to supply the muscles with extra fuel, but they can't always keep up. As a result, lactic acid accumulates in the muscles, sapping strength and literally paralyzing any further contractions.

Portable Heaters

Shivering is the body's natural warming mechanism and can actually serve as a lifesaver in extreme cold. Shivering produces heat by forcing muscles to contract and relax rapidly. About 80 percent of the muscle energy used in this process is turned into body heat—enough, in some cases, to boil a quart of water for up to an hour.

One study found shivering superior to hot water bottles or exercise when trying to warm the body. In fact, warmth from an external source may actually be harmful in cases of moderate hypothermia because it stops the shivering reflex.

Muscle-Less Fingers

The fingers are among the most frequently used parts of the body, yet they consist only of tendons. The muscles that pull these tendons are located in the hand and forearm. Roll up your sleeves and wiggle your fingers, and you'll see the contractions in the forearm.

Longest, Strongest, Largest, Smallest, Fastest, Slowest

The longest muscle in the body, the sartorius, extends from the waist to the knee and is used to flex both the hip and the knee.

The strongest muscle is the gluteus maximus ("rump"), which moves the thigh bone.

The largest is the latissimus dorsi, the flat muscle of the back that allows arm rotation.

Among the smallest is the stapedius, measuring 1/20th of an inch. It activates the stirrup that sends vibrations from the eardrum to the inner ear. Another mighty mite is the erector pili, used to raise goosebumps on the skin.

The fastest are the eye muscles, which contract in less than 1/100th of a second.

The slowest is the soleus of the lower leg, which helps keep the body in an upright position and contracts in 1/10th of a second.

It's Easier to Smile

The risorious and zygomaticus muscles work in tandem with 15 other muscles in the face to create a smile. In contrast, a frown requires 43 muscles and therefore is much more difficult to form.

Largest Biceps

The largest biceps ever recorded belong to Isaac Nessen, with a diameter of 26⅛ inches, or over 2 feet.

▼▼▼▼▼▼▼▼▼▼▼

Our
Heart &
Blood

HOW THE HEART WORKS

Little bigger than a clenched fist, the heart expands and contracts 70 times per minute in the average man (78 in a woman, 90 in a ten-year-old, and 130 in an infant), pumping an average of 1,500 gallons of blood each day. In a lifetime, the heart pumps enough blood to fill 13 supertankers, each holding one million barrels.

When questioned, most people inaccurately place the location of the heart completely in the left side of the chest. One-third of the heart, however, is situated on the right side.

The heart is divided into four chambers: the atria, which are the upper two chambers; and the ventricles, which are the lower two. Blood is pumped through these chambers with the help of four valves—the tricuspid, pulmonary, mitral, and aortic—that open and close to permit blood flow.

As blood is circulated, its oxygen and nutrient content is delivered to the cells of hungry tissues and organs. Stripped of oxygen, blood turns blue.

This blue blood eventually makes its way back to the heart (blood takes about 16 seconds to be pumped from the heart to the toes and back again), where it is received by the right atrium

135

and pumped to the lungs. In the lungs, blood exchanges its excess carbon dioxide and picks up a fresh supply of oxygen.

The left ventricle pumps this red, oxygen-rich blood into the aorta, which takes it to the rest of the 60,000 miles of the circulatory system to repeat the body-feeding process all over again.

The Athlete's Heart

Like any other muscle, the heart grows and becomes more efficient in response to exercise. The athlete's heart pumps the same amount of blood as the average person but with fewer beats. A well-conditioned heart, such as that of a marathon runner, may beat half as fast as an unconditioned heart. Listed below are heart-rate differences between certain athletes:

Athlete Type	Pulse at Rest
Average adult	70–78
Fencer	68
Weight lifter	65
Volleyball player	60
Sprinter	58
Football player	55
Oarsman	50
Swimmer/long-distance runner	40–45
Marathon runner	35

The heart increases in size and pumps more blood per beat when the body is in a horizontal position. In the water a swimmer's heart pumps even more blood per beat—as much as 20 percent more—because circulation is less impeded by the forces of gravity.

Beating Out of the Body

The heart muscle continues to beat when removed from the body. Due to the unique electrical properties of cardiac muscle cells, even tiny pieces of muscle cut from the heart will continue to pulse if placed in a test tube of warm saline.

Music to Slow the Heart By

Musical scores that approximate the rhythm of the resting heart (70 beats per minute) are most soothing to the psyche and can actually slow a heart that is beating too fast. The music found most effective in slowing an anxious heart includes:

- Venus, the Bringer of Peace *(The Planets)*, by Holst
- *Mother Goose Suite,* first movement, by Ravel
- *The Brandenburg Concertos,* no. 4, second movement, by Bach
- *Orchestral Suite,* no. 2 (Saraband), by Bach

Heart Attacks

A heart attack is the death of, or damage to, part of the heart muscle due to insufficient blood supply. This shortage of blood is most often attributed to arteries having become clogged from excessive buildup of cholesterol, or to smoking, which is known to constrict blood vessels. Most heart attacks occur between 6 and 9 A.M., when heart rate and blood pressure rise and blood platelets are "stickier" and more likely to contribute to clotting. The least number of heart attacks occur at midnight, when heart rate, blood pressure, and stress hormones fall.

THOSE RED-BLOODED HUMANS

Blood is made up of red blood cells, white blood cells, and platelets that float in the straw-colored fluid plasma. This fluid component not only accounts for 55 percent of the blood's composition but also distributes proteins, glucose, salts, vitamins, hormones, and antibodies throughout the body.

Red blood cells are the second largest component of blood, numbering 25 trillion in the average body. Each red blood cell transports oxygen molecules from the lungs and distributes them to the tissues and organs. The tissues, in turn, infuse the red blood cells with carbon dioxide, a waste product, which is carried to the lungs for expulsion. Each red blood cell circuits the body up to 300,000 times, or a period of about 120 days before wearing out and dying. Three million replacement cells, meanwhile, are manufactured in bone marrow each minute.

White blood cells, though smaller in number, have an equally important role to play. They destroy dead cells, for example, and produce antibodies to fight viruses. Some actually eat and digest bacteria. White blood cells are produced by the lymph nodes, the spleen, the thymus gland, the tonsils, and the bone marrow.

Produced in the marrow, platelets clot and mend torn blood vessels by sticking to the area around a wound but survive for only 5 to 8 days.

Blood Types
Blood is classified into four types: A, B, AB, and O.

- Type A contains the protein antigen A in the red cells and the protein antibody b in the plasma. Antigens stimulate the body to produce antibodies.
- Type B contains antigen B and antibody a.
- Type AB contains both antigens but no antibody.
- Type O has no antigens but both antibodies.

Because certain antigens and antibodies are hostile to one another, some blood types cannot be mixed. These hostile components clump together in battle and cause fatal blockages in blood vessels.

The four blood types are known to interact as follows:

- Type A can safely receive blood from types A and O.
- Type B can receive types B and O.
- Type AB are "universal recipients" and can receive all blood types.
- Type O can receive only O blood, but are "universal donors" because O is acceptable to all other blood types.
- Type O is the most common blood type worldwide.

Twice Around the Earth
If laid end-to-end, the body's blood vessels would encircle the earth more than two times.

Stacked one atop the other, the red blood cells would create a tower 31,000 miles high.

Pins and Needles
The sensation of "pins and needles" when a limb "falls asleep" is caused by impaired blood circulation.

▼▼▼▼▼▼▼▼▼▼▼

Our
Stomach &
Digestion

HOW THE STOMACH WORKS

The adult stomach has 35 million digestive glands. Stomach
acid is one of the most powerful corrosives known: it can
dissolve razor blades and other small metal objects in less than
a week. In order to avoid digesting itself with its own production of acid, the stomach must produce a new lining every 3
days. This means that the lining must shed and regenerate
about 500,000 cells every minute.

Your Digestive Timetable
Ever wonder what happens to your lunch after it disappears in your mouth? A typical meal consisting of 65 percent
carbohydrate, 25 percent protein, and 10 percent fat takes
about 4 hours after ingestion to be absorbed into the bloodstream. The following represents a typical human digestive
timetable:

12 Noon.   Meal begins. With its 9,000 taste buds, the
mouth and tongue analyze the first bite of food and identify it
in 1/10th of a second. Teeth chop up and soften food, with

molars clamping down with a force equal to 150 pounds or more. Meanwhile, saliva glands make digestive juice. Food is swallowed and passes into the esophagus. (Even if you stand on your head while eating, the contracting muscles of the esophagus will still pull the food up into the stomach.)

12:01. First food drops into stomach. Acids and enzymes break down food into fragments, creating a soupy consistency called "chyme." Stomach contractions churn and mix the chyme every 20 seconds. When finished processing, food moves into the small intestine (a 15- to 25-foot tube), where most digestion and absorption into the bloodstream take place.

1 P.M. The pancreas secretes alkaline digestive juices into the intestine to neutralize any stomach acid remaining on food. (About a quart of alkaline is used for this purpose each day.) The liver and gallbladder add bile to help break up fats. Other enzymes and chemicals are secreted onto the food by the intestine itself. Through complex muscle contractions, the small intestine churns, kneads, and segments the food. When processing is complete, nutrients pass through the wall of the small intestine and enter blood and lymph vessels to be transported to the liver and other organs.

The liver performs many important functions at this time: it absorbs and stores such nutrients as iron, copper, and several fat-soluble vitamins; it detoxifies poisons in the blood and removes waste products; it manufactures glycogen to stabilize the body's blood-sugar levels; and it produces bile, a yellowish-green liquid used in the digestion of fats. The gallbladder located beneath the liver acts as a storage sac for bile.

In addition to producing alkaline and digestive enzymes, the pancreas also manufactures insulin to help regulate blood-sugar levels in the body.

5 P.M. Undigested food enters the large intestine where most of the water is absorbed. The large intestine pushes waste products toward the rectum for later removal.

The kidneys, meanwhile, help remove poisonous waste products in the blood by recirculating nutrients and regulating the body's water supply. Collected waste is turned into the sterile liquid known as urine which, while still in the body and as yet unexposed to outside bacteria, is cleaner than saliva. The urine then flows to the bladder for storage.

As the bladder fills, the added pressure stretches tiny sense organs within the bladder wall, sending a message to the brain that elimination is necessary.

8 A.M. Food wastes are prepared to leave the large intestine. Approximately 150 grams of feces are eliminated from the body each day—equivalent to 120 pounds per year, or 9,000 pounds within a lifetime. These waste products consist of 100 grams of water and 50 grams of bacteria, including undigested cellulose, cell debris, bile pigments, and salt.

HARD TO STOMACH

Intestinal Gas
The average human expels about a pint of intestinal gas per day in the form of flatulence. Between 30 and 50 percent of this

gas is caused by fermentation of undigested food; the remaining 50 to 70 percent results from swallowed air.

Flatulence caused by fermentation has an odor almost universally experienced as unpleasant, while gas produced by swallowed air has no odor.

The odor-causing agents in escaping gas are ammonia, hydrogen sulfide, amino acids, fatty acids, and the extremely odiferous amines, such as indole and skatole. Ironically, both of these compounds are used in the manufacture of perfumes, particularly violet-scented ones.

The all-time worst gas producers are chewing gum, carbonated soft drinks, apple juice, beans, broccoli, cabbage, cauliflower, brussels sprouts, and turnips.

Vomiting

Receptors in the stomach wall send nerve impulses to the "vomiting center" of the brain when dangerous bacteria or viruses are present in food or, frequently, when we overeat. The brain relays impulses back, causing the muscles of the stomach and esophagus to relax. The muscles of the diaphragm and abdomen then contract in a powerful spasm, ejecting food from the stomach. Sometimes the pyloric sphincter opens, and some of the small intestine's contents may also be ejected.

FACTS ABOUT FOOD

Food and Height

According to a study of primary students in England, those picky eaters who shun healthy foods as children may grow up to stand an inch shorter than their less fussy peers. Researchers found that the less variety of food a child ate, the more severe the loss in potential height. With children who avoided three or more foods, the deficit was as high as 1½ inches.

Food for Thought

The types of food we eat also affect the brain. Children with diets high in sugar, for example, score lower on IQ tests and perform more poorly in school than do their better nourished peers. Carbohydrates elevate brain serotonin, causing drowsiness and lowered sensitivity to pain; protein, on the other hand, lowers serotonin and increases alertness.

How Much Do We Eat?

To feed an American in an average lifetime, the following shopping list will take care of the essentials:

4 tons beef	½ ton cheese
4 tons potatoes	108,000 slices bread
4 tons fresh vegetables	2,900 gallons soda
3 tons fresh fruit	2,000 gallons milk
2 tons chicken	1,800 gallons beer
½ ton fish	880 gallons tea
20,000 eggs	296 gallons wine
3½ tons sugar	80,000 cups coffee

The typical North American puts away about a ton of food and drink per year. That's a lifetime total of nearly 74 tons.

Eating Around the World
Approximately 45 percent of humans worldwide eat with knives, forks, and spoons; 36 percent manage with chopsticks; 11 percent eat with hands and a knife; and 8 percent eat only with the hands alone.

Body Input/Output Over Lifetime
The direct and indirect results of our ingesting an estimated 74 tons of food over a lifetime reveals the following rather overwhelming totals:

Function	Lifetime Totals
Quarts of urine expelled	40,515
Heartbeats	2,700,000,000
Quarts of blood pumped	350,000,000
Breaths taken	740,000,000
Sperm produced	400,000,000,000
Eggs produced	400
Eye blinks	333,000,000
Finger joint flexes	25,000,000
Hair growth (scalp)	350 miles
Nail growth	12 feet per finger
Laughs	540,000
Cries	3,000
Dreams/nightmares	127,500

900 Miles to the Gallon
The human body is incredibly efficient at turning food into fuel. For example, to ride a bicycle for an hour at 10 miles per hour, the body needs the food energy contained in only 3 ounces of carbohydrate—roughly the equivalent of 1.4 ounces of gasoline. If our bodies used gasoline instead of food, we could ride over 900 miles on a single gallon of gas.

In the body, a pound of butter creates 3 times as much energy as a pound of TNT, a highly toxic and flammable compound.

NUTRITION AND HEALTH CONSIDERATIONS

A Food/Weight Breakdown

Every pound of body weight equals 3,500 calories. If we eat 500 calories more per day than we expend through activity, we'll gain a pound by the end of a week, or 52 pounds by the end of a year.

For many people it's just as difficult to gain weight as it is to lose it. In general, the typical human must eat about 39 potatoes to gain one pound of weight. With chocolate cake, of course, weight gain comes easier, as illustrated below.

Food	Amount Needed to Gain One Pound
Celery stalk	700*
Tomato (small)	117
Apple	50
Bread slice	50
Banana	41
Potato	39
Pear	35
Frankfurter	23
Whole milk	22 cups
T-bone steak	1½ pounds
Chocolate cake with chocolate frosting (16 inches in diameter)	1

*This assumes that no calories are burned while eating the celery. In reality, the body uses more calories in chewing and swallowing a stalk than it gets back.

Dieting and Exercise

The first weight a dieter loses consists largely of water, not fat. Continued dieting sends a message to the brain to slow metabolism, so that calories are burned less quickly. This is an evolutionary adaptation to help protect us in times of famine and also the reason why losing weight can be so difficult.

Exercise, on the other hand, speeds up metabolism so that body fat is shed faster. Exercise is also known to suppress appetite.

Based on a U.S. Sports Academy study, the chart below indicates the best exercises for burning calories.

Activity	Calories Burned per Hour
Cross-country skiing	1,000
Running (10 mph)	900
Swimming	750
Bicycling (13 mph)	660
Handball	550
Tennis (singles)	450
Table tennis	350
Walking (3½ mph)	300

The Ultimate Diet

The longest humans can survive without food is about 60 days. The world record for fasting is 382 days, but the feat was only possible with vitamin and liquid supplements.

Without liquids, the average human can only hold out about 6 days. Unlike nutrients, water cannot be stored for long periods of time. Although we drink about 3 quarts of liquid each day, about 2½ quarts are lost daily as urine, perspiration, and breath.

TASTE

The average adult has 9,000 taste buds on the surfaces of the tongue, roof of the mouth, and throat. Children have several taste buds in their cheeks, which disappear at adolescence.

Each bud has tiny receptor cells tipped with hairs that transmit four basic flavors through nerves leading to the brain. The buds on the tip of the tongue are sensitive to sweetness. Those at the tongue's upper front portion respond to salty tastes. The sour buds are concentrated mainly along the sides of the tongue, while the bitter ones are located in the back. These bitter-tasting buds are 10,000 times more sensitive than the sweet buds, a necessary adaptation to help alert us to poisonous substances.

The spectrum of flavors we experience are created by a combination of food temperature, texture, and odor, along with taste-bud sensation.

Odor plays one of the most important roles in how we perceive flavor. A potato, for example, tastes almost identical to an apple when smell is blocked. Studies also show the impossibility of distinguishing between the taste of different meats without the use of smell.

Our Aging Taste Buds

Taste buds begin to atrophy after the age of 45, and flavor perception drops significantly. This is why older people often go heavier on the seasonings than younger people.

Animal Taste Buds

Even though humans eat the widest variety of foods, many animals have considerably more taste buds, as illustrated below:

Animal	Tastebuds
Catfish	100,000
Cow	35,000
Rabbit	17,000
Pig	15,000
Goat	15,000
Human	9,000
Bat	800
Bird	200 or less

Our
Lungs &
Breathing

HOW THE LUNGS WORK

The lungs are two spongelike organs consisting of 3 lobes, or sections, on the right and two lobes on the left. Air entering through the nose or mouth is sucked down through the trachea and into the deepest parts of the lungs through the tracheobronchial tree, which resembles an inverted tree. The "tree" branches out into thousands of small tubes and subdivides further into millions of smaller bronchioles. At the end of each bronchiole are alveoli, tiny air sacs through which blood and oxygen are diffused. Each alveoli measures only 1/250,000th of an inch thick.

Once every minute the heart pumps the body's entire blood supply through the lungs. Through capillary action, the alveoli soak up blue, oxygen-depleted blood and remove its carbon dioxide, a waste product. The blue blood is then infused with fresh oxygen, which turns the blood red again. This oxygenated blood is then pumped back through the body to feed hungry tissues, while the carbon dioxide is expelled by an exhale.

151

Surface Area of the Lungs

The total surface area of the lungs is roughly the size of a tennis court, providing enough space for some 300 billion capillaries. If stretched end to end, these capillaries would reach from New York to Florida.

Origin of the Lungs

The evolution of the lungs can be traced directly to fish. Scientists speculate that lungs probably began as throat pouches on ancient fish to help them take in air in swampy areas where the water was low in oxygen. These throat pouches later helped fish adapt to living out of the water entirely, paving the way for the evolution of air-breathing amphibians and reptiles.

Lung Capacity

Lung capacity—or how much air we can breathe in and expel—is an excellent indicator of how long we'll live. Non-smokers and those who regularly exercise their lungs are most likely to live the longest.

LIFE AND BREATH

Baby's First Breath

To fill its lungs for the first time, a newborn must create a suction 50 times more powerful than that of an average adult breath.

Air Requirements

The body requires 8 quarts of air per minute when lying down, 16 quarts when sitting, 24 quarts when walking, and 50 or more quarts when running. In a lifetime, the average person will breathe about 75 million gallons of air.

City Air and Ancient Air

City dwellers breathe in some 20 million particles of foreign matter each day. Evidence suggests that even ancient man breathed polluted air. Carbon deposits—from inhaling wood smoke in unventilated homes—are commonly found in the lungs of preserved mummies.

153

Holding Our Breath Longer

We can hold our breath longer by breathing deeply for one minute and saturating the lungs with oxygen before holding it. Professional swimmers can hold their breath three times as long as usual this way.

Breathing Sunbeams

Through the process of photosynthesis, plants convert solar energy into nutrients and release oxygen into the atmosphere. Scientifically speaking, then, the air we breathe is little more than an altered form of sunbeams.

The world's largest supply of oxygen lies in the world's largest forest, the Amazon Jungle.

Slow-Breathing Oldsters

The older we get, the slower we breathe, as illustrated below:

Age	Breaths per Minute
Infant	40–60
5 years	24–26
15 years	20–22
25 years* (male)	14–18
25 years* (female)	16–20

*Breathing levels off after the age of 25.

Smoker's Woes

A typical male smoker can expect to die at age 67. A two-pack-a-day smoker will likely die at 60, compared to 74 for nonsmokers. For each pack of cigarettes smoked per day, life expectancy is lowered by 7 years.

PART
4

OUR
BEGINNING
&
END

Our
Conception
& Infancy

OUR GENESIS

The ovaries of every human female at birth contain some two million eggs, each carrying a genetic code adapted from thousands of generations of human breeding. Of the 300,000 eggs that survive to puberty, about 450 are ultimately released for possible fertilization during a woman's reproductive years. The egg is the largest of the body's cells and the only one that can be seen with the naked eye.

The smallest of the body's cells, on the other hand, are the male's sperm cells, each about 1/500th of an inch long. The testes manufacture 15 billion sperm cells each month, and 400 million sperm are released in a single ejaculation. In addition to the 22 chromosomes that carry the father's genetic blueprints, each sperm carries either an X or Y sex chromosome. The X determines a female; the Y, a male.

Prolific Moms
The human female is designed to produce as many as 35 children in her lifetime. By comparison, the Multimammate rat of Africa may produce as many as 120 pups each year.

157

This biological limit for humans is occasionally surpassed, however, as was the case of a Soviet woman who gave birth to a record 69 children. In 27 pregnancies between 1725 and 1765, she bore 16 pairs of twins, 7 sets of triplets, and 4 sets of quadruplets. Of these children, 67 actually survived infancy, according to a Moscow report.

The world's most prolific mothers today are Kenyans, who bear an average of 8 children. Europeans, by contrast, produce an average of 2 children or less. The worldwide average is 4 children.

Old Moms

Statistics reveal that 7,558 American women over the age of 45 gave birth in 1940. In 1985, only 1,162 women over age 45 gave birth, testifying to the effectiveness of contraception in modern times.

The oldest mother on record is Mrs. Ruth Kistler of Oregon, who gave birth to a healthy daughter at age 57½.

Teen Pregnancy

Contrary to popular opinion, teenage pregnancy has remained relatively stable in this century. As evidenced in the chart below, there were actually more teen pregnancies in the 1950s and 1970s than in the 1980s.

Year	Number of Pregnancies
1940	336,532
1955	499,951
1970	656,460
1985	477,705

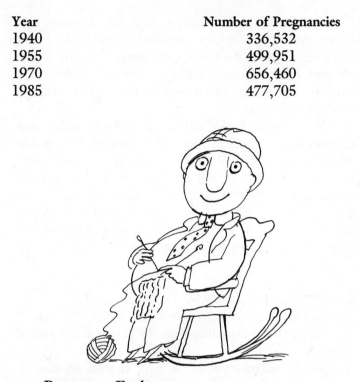

Pregnant Fathers

Husbands often display the same symptoms as their expectant wives. For example, it's not unusual for husbands to suffer from morning sickness to the point of vomiting. According to a study at Case Western Reserve, 40 percent of "psychologically pregnant" men suffer mood changes and weight gain during their mate's pregnancy. The average weight gain is 4 pounds, but some men may put on as much as 25 additional pounds.

The Dispensable Male

In the future, males may not be needed for successful reproduction. In fact, there are many organisms that reproduce successfully without engaging in sex.

Parthenogenesis—reproduction without the use of sperm—occurs in fish, reptiles, amphibians, and birds, but it has never been known to occur in mammals. In the southwestern part of the United States, 12 species of lizard are known to have produced seven generations without males, a literal "clone of animals."

A Yale University biologist has attempted to induce parthenogenetic development in mice, but to no avail. It's possible to start the development of a mammalian egg without sperm by electrical shock, mechanical agitation, or by adding a salt solution, but the embryo always dies before going halfway through gestation. This may be an evolutionary developed mechanism meant to ensure continued use of sexual reproduction, with the long-term benefits of genetic variation that result.

Constructing a Human From Scratch
A human begins life as a single-celled zygote, the merged sperm and egg, which is smaller than the period at the end of this sentence.

This single cell contains all the necessary information to create and build a human from scratch. The cell ultimately divides into more than 100 trillion sister cells, some forming the eyes, some the veins and arteries, and others the organs, and so on. The method by which these cells "know" how to organize themselves into something as complex as a heart or a tongue remains a mystery.

Even after the first month of pregnancy, the human embryo is still small enough to fit on a quarter. By the third month, it could easily fit into a large hen's egg. More than half of a fetus's birth weight comes in the last 6 to 8 weeks of development.

The Ghosts of Our Ancestors
The developing embryo of a human and a dog are remarkably similar. Both have tiny gill arches—evidence that we once

lived in the sea. The arches are found near the neck, similar to fish. But in humans, as in the dog and other mammals, the arches transform to become the skeleton of the larynx and muscles of the face.

Both the dog and human embryo have tiny tails as well; in humans, the tail diminishes before birth. Occasionally an infant is born with a full-fledged tail, which must be surgically removed.

During the sixth month of development in the womb, the ghosts of our ancestors continue to appear, as the human fetus is protectively covered with lanugo, a fine coat of fur. Like the tail, lanugo also disappears before birth.

The Fetal Sea

Amniotic fluid is derived from a mixture of maternal blood and fetal urine that is replaced every 3 hours. Between the eighth and twelfth week the urine is formed, which the fetus then drinks, expels into the amniotic fluid, and drinks again.

The Conscious Fetus

Fetuses become conscious during the second trimester of pregnancy. From the fourth month on, the unborn child is easily startled and turns away when a bright light is flashed on its mother's belly. By six months, the fetus is reacting to sounds. Studies show, for example, that soothing music calms the fetus, while rock music initiates frantic kicking. Emotionally, the fetus appears to react to its inner thought processes as well: at six months it can be seen frowning, grimacing, and smiling.

As they develop in the months to follow, fetuses may suck their thumbs hard enough to raise blisters. Ultrasound exams clearly reveal erections in males now as well.

Listed below are gestation periods of various animals as compared to those of a human's:

Animal	Gestation Period (days)
Indian elephant	625
Rhinoceros	560
Giraffe	410
Camel	400
Whale	365
Horse	340
Cow	280
Human	266
Chimpanzee	237
Goat	151
Dog	63
Cat	60
Rabbit	30
Mouse	19
Hamster	16
Opossum	12

OH, BABY!

Born on the Graveyard Shift

Due to the body's natural time clocks, more babies are born between midnight and 8 A.M. than at any other time. For mysterious reasons, more babies are born on a Tuesday in the United States (see the chart below).

Average Births During a Seven-Day Week	
Sunday	8,532
Monday	10,243
Tuesday	10,730
Wednesday	10,515
Thursday	10,476
Friday	10,514
Saturday	8,799

Only 1 out of 20 babies is born on the day predicted by its obstetrician.

In the Merry Month of May

Babies born in May weigh an average of 6 ounces more than babies born in any other month.

Full-Moon Babies

More babies are born under a full moon than any other time in the lunar cycle.

Brunette versus Blond

Brunette mothers deliver slightly faster than blond mothers. Boys are delivered slightly faster than girls are.

Baby Blues and Browns

All babies are born with blue eyes, regardless of race. Pigment changes—sometimes within hours of birth—as the baby develops. Most humans, in fact, end up with brown eyes.

Contrary to folklore, blue-eyed parents don't always produce blue-eyed children. The numbers, according to a Danish study, are as follows:

	Number of Children		
Parent	*Blue*	*Brown*	*Gray-Green / Blue-Green*
Blue-eyed father/ blue-eyed mother	625	12	7
Blue-eyed father/ brown-eyed mother	317	322	9
Brown-eyed father/ blue-eyed mother	25	82	—

Hearing Dad, Sniffing Out Mom

A newborn can differentiate the sound of its father's voice from that of the delivering obstetrician. The identification factor appears to be strongest with a father who "talks" with the fetus before birth.

Within six days after birth, a newborn can identify its mother by smell alone. In tests, an infant invariably turns toward the scent of its mother while shunning that of a stranger.

Remembering Birth

Babies may be so aware that they can recall the events of their birth years later under hypnosis. At least two studies show that it is possible to remember birth experiences. During his years as an obstetrician, one doctor kept careful records of birth procedures under lock and key for twenty years. He then contacted the young men and women he had delivered two decades before, hypnotized them, and asked them to recall specific details of their births. Their recollections matched the details described in their birth records with remarkable precision. A similar study was later conducted by a clinical psychologist who claimed his subjects remembered their mother's hairstyle and emotional state, the surgical instruments used, and even conversations among hospital attendants.

Most people are unable to recall distant memories because birth produces an amnesiac effect. Oxytocin, the female hormone secreted during labor to induce uterine contractions, has been shown to cause amnesia in animals, and may affect human babies the same way. Hypnosis appears to be the only way to crack the amnesiac code.

INFANT DEVELOPMENT

Miraculous Mother's Milk

Human milk contains the same amount of fat, half the protein, and twice the sugar of cow's milk. Although growth rates for bottle-fed and breast-fed babies are the same, human milk contains superior immunological properties. Antibodies for mumps, polio, influenza, vaccinia, salmonella, streptococci, herpes simplex, and Japanese encephalitis are all passed on to the newborn's immune system through breast milk of the mother.

Hugging and Infant Growth
Infants can actually die without regular stroking and holding. Cuddling and caressing stimulates respiration, blood flow, and growth rate. Hugged babies are healthier, grow faster, cry less, and are more active.

Rocking Baby's Brain
Science has discovered that gently rocking a baby stimulates its cerebellum, the part of the brain involved in coordination. In fact, the more rocking a baby has, the faster it matures. Vision, sleep cycles, and even growth rates improve with periodic rocking.

Temperaments
Difficult infants—those with angry or moody temperaments—grow up to suffer more emotional problems later in life. Of the difficult babies surveyed in one study, 70 percent required psychiatric counseling in childhood or adolescence, while only 18 percent of "easygoing" babies did.

According to a similar study, a pregnant woman in a bad marriage has over a 200 percent greater chance of giving birth to a child with physical or psychological problems.

Baby Teeth
Only 1 in 2,000 infants is born with a tooth already showing. Julius Caesar, Hannibal, and Napoleon were among these rare infants.

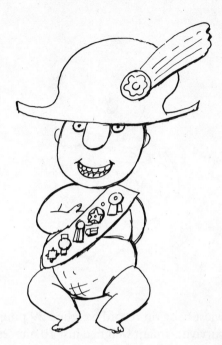

Baby Tears

Chinese babies cry less and are more easily consoled than American ones.

Most newborns cry without tears until they are 3 to 6 weeks old.

Malnourished babies and brain-damaged babies cry a full octave higher than well-fed, healthy ones.

Brutes and Pint-sized Babies

Nearly 95 percent of newborns tip the scales at between 5½ and 10 pounds. The average Caucasian boy born in the United States weighs 7½ pounds; the average girl, 7.4. Nonwhite babies weigh slightly less.

The heaviest baby on record weighed 29 pounds at birth. The lightest surviving infant weighed just 10 ounces when born prematurely, and was fed with a fountain-pen filler.

Drinking Dads Produce More Girls
Heavy-drinking men are ten times more likely to sire girls, because alcohol diminishes the male testosterone levels responsible for producing boys.

Twins, Triplets, Quindecaplets
Women are more likely to bear twins and triplets as their age increases (older women frequently release more than one egg each month), and their odds of conception decreases. Thirty percent of women between the ages of 35 and 39 are unable to conceive, yet women in this age group typically have the most multiple births. On July 22, 1971, a doctor removed a record 15 fetuses—10 girls, 5 boys—from the womb of a 35-year-old housewife who had been using a fertility drug. This is the only case of "quindecaplets" in history.

168

In the United States, Asians have the most fraternal twins, with 1 in 40 births; whites have the least, with 1 in 100. Blacks are in the median range, with 1 in 77.

The number of twin births has increased in the last decade due to several factors: first, many women are having babies later in life; and second, there has been a marked increase in the use of fertility drugs and out-of-womb fertilization.

There were 79,500 twins born in the United States in 1986, or 21.6 per 1,000 babies, while in 1980 the number of twins was 68,340, or 19.3 per 1,000 births.

Triplets, meanwhile, occur in 1 out of every 7,744 pregnancies, and quadruplets occur in 1 out of every 681,472 pregnancies.

Yearning for a Lost Twin

Many a "singleton" is actually a surviving twin. Among a small portion of early detected twin pregnancies, only one infant develops and is born, while the other is resorbed by the body.

Circumcision

The oldest known surgical procedure is removal of the foreskin from the penis, or circumcision. The practice has been carried out by Jews, Moslems, and some African tribes for centuries. In the 1960s, 95 percent of U.S. male infants were circumcised. This procedure dropped sharply, however, in the 1970s after studies suggested there were no valid medical reasons for performing the surgery. Then, in 1989, the American Academy of Pediatrics cited a new study, showing that the procedure protects against infections of the kidneys and urinary system. In the study, uncircumcised boys in the first year of life were 11 times more likely to suffer urinary tract infections than boys who had the foreskin removed.

Our
Life Span

THE DAYS OF OUR LIVES

The maximum life span for a human is generally accepted to be
110 years. A few people have reportedly lived beyond this age
but had little or no documentation to prove their true birth
years. One exception, however, is Shigechiyo Izumi, a Japanese
man who was born undisputably on June 29, 1865. Japan's first
census of 1871 recorded Izumi as a 6-year-old at the time. At
the age of 119, the world's oldest man attributed his longevity
to leaving things to "God, the Sun, and Buddha." Izumi died
in 1986 at the age of 120.

    The list below shows maximum human life span compared
to those of other living creatures:

Creature	Maximum Life Span (years)
Bristlecone pine	4,600+
Quahog (clam)	150
Tortoise	138
Human	120
Blue whale	95
Asiatic elephant	78
Condor	72
Orangutan	59

(continued)

Creature	Maximum Life Span (years)
Hippo	51
Ostrich	50
Horse	46
Gorilla	39
Cat	34
Mouse	8
Earthworm	6
Housefly	76 days

The list below shows typical life spans of yesteryear:

Time Period	Life Span (years)
Neanderthal	18–29 (varied estimates)
Mesolithic	22
Greece (400 B.C.)	30
Rome A.D. (600)	30
Anglo-Saxon (800)	31
England (1250)	35
United States (1750)	36
England (1850)	40
England (1940)	60
England (1961)	71
United States (1980)	73.8
United States (1988)	74.7

LONGEVITY FACTORS

Age

Our projected life span increases as we get older. A 60-year-old American woman can expect to live to age 82½. If she reaches 85, her projected life span moves up to 91. The rate of increase for men is slightly less.

Race
In America, whites generally outlive blacks. However, a reversal occurs when a white woman and a black woman reach old age: a black woman over the age of 70 almost always outlives her white counterpart.

Height
Short people typically outlive their taller peers by as much as 10 percent.

Blood Type
Men with type O blood live longer than men with type B blood, but the exact opposite is true with women.

Childbearing
Single women have the highest life expectancy of all groups. Women who have had children live longer and suffer significantly fewer heart attacks than women who remain childless.

Exercise
Each stair you climb adds 4 seconds to your life, according to studies at Johns Hopkins University.

Vocation
Nuns enjoy the longest life spans in most modernized nations. Mormons and Seventh-Day Adventists have the next longest life spans. Each of these groups abstain from alcohol and tobacco. Following close behind are the professionals—doctors, lawyers, and so on. Contrary to popular belief, unskilled laborers suffer the highest stress levels of all workers and have the shortest life spans. Unmarried and unskilled laborers typically have the shortest life spans of all.

A study by a major insurance company reveals that baseball players tend to outlive the rest of the population. Among the ballplayers, third basemen have the longest life spans and shortstops and catchers the shortest.

The following overview of life spans in the United States—ranging from longest to shortest—further categorizes these segments of our population:

Who Lives the Longest?
1. Nuns of medium or small build
2. Nuns of larger build
3. Mormons and Seventh-Day Adventists of medium or small build
4. Mormons and Seventh-Day Adventists of larger build
5. Small or shorter women
6. Professionals (doctors, lawyers, etc.)
7. Semiprofessionals (managerial positions and other occupations with status and control over others and the work itself)
8. Short unskilled laborers, married

9. Tall unskilled laborers, married
10. Unskilled laborers, unmarried
11. Unskilled laborers, divorced
12. Tall, unskilled, alcoholic laborers, divorced

Professional Singing

Singing conditions the muscles used in respiration, thus increasing lung capacity. A study by the National Institute on Aging found that professional singers, and particularly opera singers, have the healthiest lungs in America and outlive the rest of the population by as much as 20 years.

Environment

Women outlive men in nearly every nation on earth. The average female living in Japan, the healthiest nation, can expect to survive for 80½ years, while her male compatriots succumb more than 5½ years earlier. Conversely, females in India often die by the age of 52, while Indian males outlive them by only 4 months.

Although the worldwide average life span is 60 years, the diversity from country to country is significant indeed, as illustrated in years below:

Male Life Expectancy		Female Life Expectancy	
Japan	74.8	Japan	80.5
Sweden	73.8	Switzerland	80.0
Switzerland	73.5	Sweden	79.7
Israel	73.1	Netherlands	79.7
Netherlands	72.9	Norway	79.5
Norway	72.8	France	79.2
Spain	72.6	Canada	79.0
Australia	72.3	Australia	78.8
Cyprus	72.3	Spain	78.6
Greece	72.2	Finland	78.5
Canada	71.9	United States	78.2
England	71.8	West Germany	77.8
Denmark	71.6	Italy	77.8
United States	71.2	England	77.7

The shortest life spans are as follows:

Male (years)		Female (years)	
Ecuador	59.5	Ecuador	61.8
Pakistan	59.0	Peru	60.5
Peru	56.8	Egypt	59.5
Egypt	56.8	Guatemala	59.4
Iran	55.8	Pakistan	59.2
Guatemala	55.1	South Africa	55.2
Bangladesh	54.9	Iran	55.0
India	52.5	Kenya	54.7
South Africa	51.8	Bangladesh	54.7
Kenya	51.2	India	52.1

Between 1965 and 1980, life expectancy in the USSR dropped from 66.2 years to 61.9 for males and from 74.1 to 73.5 for females. The U.S. Census Bureau reports that the death rate from alcohol poisoning in the USSR has become 88 times higher than that in the United States.

Under the Doctor's Influence

According to at least three independent surveys, the human death rate invariably decreases whenever doctors go on strike. In 1976, for example, doctors in Los Angeles went on strike to protest the skyrocketing cost of malpractice insurance. An 18 percent drop in the death rate was recorded during the strike. In that same year, doctors in Bogota, Colombia, refused to handle all but the most urgent cases: the rate of death plummeted 35 percent. When Israeli doctors began limiting their patient contact in 1973, 50 percent fewer deaths occurred.

Most authorities cite unnecessary surgery as the prime culprit behind the phenomenon. Perhaps of equal importance is what physicians refer to as nosocomial or "hospital" disease. While being treated for one disease, over 1 million patients annually in the United States contract a second disease caused by the hospital environment itself; of these, 15,000 succumb to the hospital-borne ailment. Physicians' negligence, meanwhile, kills or injures more than 100,000 patients a year, according to the Public Citizen Health Research Group.

HOW WE SPEND OUR LIVES

- 24½ years sleeping
- 13½ years at work and school
- 12 years watching TV
- 4½ years socializing

- 3 years reading
- 3 years eating
- 1¾ years bathing and grooming
- 1 year on the telephone
- 9½ months on the toilet
- 5 months having sex
- 9½ years miscellaneous activity: housekeeping, shopping, waiting in lines, walking, driving, entertainment, doing nothing

Most people will walk 115,000 miles in their lifetime, or around the world 4½ times. The average American holding a driver's license for 50 years will drive 600,000 miles, enough to circle the earth nearly 24 times.

ALL ABOUT AGING

The Incredible Shrinking Human

After age 30, weakening muscles in the back and stomach are overpowered by the force of gravity, which gradually compresses the disks between the bones of the spine, resulting in a decrease in height. How much we'll shrink over the years depends on the degree to which we keep ourselves in shape. Here are some average shrinkage profiles to ponder:

Men		Women	
Age	Height	Age	Height
30	5'10"	30	5'4¼"
40	5'9⅞"	40	5'3¾"
50	5'9⅝"	50	5'3¼"
60	5'9¼"	60	5'2¾"
70	5'8⅞"	70	5'2¼"

Life in the Slow Lane

After age 19, walking speed slows down by 1 to 2 percent each decade. After age 63, a woman slows her pace by 12.3 percent per decade, while a man gears down by 16.1 percent. Arthritis and circulatory problems are largely to blame for the slowdown.

The Aging Heart

As the heart ages, it pumps less blood with each beat. For years it was thought that such loss of pumping power was a natural effect of aging. New studies, however, show that people who stay in top physical condition may not lose any heart-pumping power whatsoever, even at age 70. The average sedentary American nevertheless shows a decline in pumping ability as early as age 30.

Age	Quarts of Blood Pumped per Minute (heart at rest)	Peak Heart Rate per Minute (during exercise)
30	3.6	200
40	3.4	182
50	3.2	171
60	2.9	159
70	2.6	150

Lung Capacity

Among men, vital lung capacity drops 1 percent a year. Between the ages of 30 and 75, for example, the volume of air that can be taken in and expelled by the lungs decreases by 45 percent. Meanwhile, the amount of oxygen passing into the blood drops by about 50 percent. Many physicians believe these factors can be delayed or even reversed simply by strengthening the muscles of the rib cage and diaphragm.

Boning Up on Old Bones

Bones thin and weaken with each passing decade, especially in women. More than 25 percent of elderly women suffer bone fractures due to osteoporosis, the thinning of bones due to a loss of calcium. Women over 50 are twice as likely as men to break their hips. By age 60, 10 times as many women as men suffer wrist fractures due to this condition.

Kidney Reserves

Of all the major internal organs, the kidneys show the greatest deterioration with age: their capacity to filter waste decreases by 50 percent by age 80. However, humans have four times the necessary reserve of kidney tissue to maintain normal function. Even with a 60 percent loss of capacity, the kidneys can still adequately perform their job.

Faltering Frequencies

Humans begin to lose the ability to hear high-frequency sound as early as childhood, although the decline usually goes unnoticed until late middle age or even older. Few people at age 65 hear sounds with frequencies of 10,000 cycles per second or higher. With this limited hearing range, it is difficult to identify voices over the telephone or to understand the speech of children. Such hearing problems affect 25 percent of the over-65 population. Hearing loss can often be prevented or delayed, however, by avoiding exposure to loud noise.

Eyeing the Future

The lenses of the eyes continually harden and thicken throughout life, causing visual acuity to decline. By age 40, many people find it difficult to focus in on close objects. At age 50, deterioration continues more rapidly. Depth perception—as well as peripheral and night vision—decrease. Between the ages of 60 and 70, yellowing of the lenses filters out the shorter wavelengths of light, making it harder to distinguish between blues and greens; and black, gray, and dark brown become equally difficult to differentiate. By age 70 or 80, the eyes take 3 times as long to adjust to the dark as at age 25.

At age 75, only 1 in 7 people has 20/20 vision, even with glasses.

Hair-Raising Experience

Thinning and graying of hair is thought to be caused by a combination of hormonal action and loss of blood flow to the scalp. For some men, hair may start to thin or even fall out as early as age 20. Thickness of hair in men is measured in microns, as illustrated below:

Age	Microns
20	101
30	98
40	96
50	94
60	86
70	80

Skin

Collagen fibers in skin break down and lose elasticity as we age. The more collagen that breaks down, the more wrinkles and lines are likely to form. Sunlight, alcohol, cigarettes, insomnia, and frowning are all known to speed up the wrinkling process. It has been estimated to take about 200,000 frowns to create just one permanent brow wrinkle.

A Growing Nose

The cartilage in the nose continues to grow as we age. Between the ages of 30 and 70, the nose grows a half-inch wider and longer. (The earlobes also grow a quarter-inch longer.)

Taste and Smell

If that steak doesn't taste as good as it once did, blame it on aging taste buds. By age 60, most people will have lost 50 percent of their taste buds and 40 percent of their ability to smell. Loss of taste buds can be delayed by avoiding alcohol, tobacco, and extremely hot foods.

Teeth and Gums

Gum disease will cause tooth loss in most people by the age of 60; however, it is related more to neglect of proper hygiene than to the aging process and can easily be prevented. One hundred years ago, 75 percent of American women over the age of 50 had no teeth. Today, the typical 70-year-old has lost only 10 teeth.

Sex

Most older couples enjoy sex into their sixties and beyond. During the teen years, males can maintain erections for 1 hour or more; in old age, however, the duration drops to about 7 minutes. Young women take just 30 seconds of sexual stimulation to begin lubrication; women over 60, on the other hand, take up to 3 minutes.

In general, sexual interest begins to decline after middle age. The peak of sexual desire for men is age 20, with interest dropping sharply after 70. Women peak at age 28 and begin a gradual decline after 45.

Sleep

Children and adolescents enjoy the soundest sleep of all age groups. Men begin having difficulty sleeping in their late twenties. Women generally don't begin to experience this difficulty until they reach menopause, when awakening once or more during the night becomes common. Physicians believe a change in the body's internal clock makes it increasingly difficult to sleep undisturbed for long periods as we get older. Nagging physical ailments may also keep the elderly awake longer. In any event, sleep duration declines (as shown below) with each passing decade.

Age	Hours
25	8
40	7½
50	6
60	5½

Calling All Memories

Many older people easily remember obscure events from childhood but forget what they had for lunch a few hours ago. This is not only normal but also common to all age groups. Contrary to popular belief, few elderly people suffer severe memory loss, where daily functions are seriously impaired. Indeed, only 15 percent of those over age 65 are plagued with the disorientation and confusion known as "senile dementia." Statistics showing the average word recall for both the young and old support this point:

Age	Words Remembered
20	14 of 25
30	13 of 24
40	11 of 24
50	10 of 24
60	9 of 24
70	7 of 24

GOOD NEWS ABOUT OLD AGE

Mental Stability

Some mental factors actually improve with age. Alcohol abuse, affective disorders, and antisocial personality are seen twice as often in people under 45 as compared to older age groups.

Aches and Pains

Teenagers are 50 percent more susceptible to colds than people over 50. Although the elderly feel the sensation of cold more acutely due to diminished circulation and changes in body fat, and are more prone to arthritis-related aches, the young often have more pain-oriented complaints. Those age 18 to 24 suffer 35 percent more headaches, 31 percent more stomach pain, 22 percent more dental pain, 20 percent more muscle pain, and 14 percent more backaches than those age 65 or older.

Our
Demise

DEALING WITH DEATH

Death Facts

The fear of death actually lessens with age. Between the ages of 45 and 54, people fear death the most; those age 65 to 74 exhibit the least fear.

Most deaths in the United States do not occur in the home: 80 percent of all deaths occur in the hospital; 70 percent of Americans who die each year are over age 65; and 5 percent who die are under age 15.

Cremation

The Japanese cremate 93 percent of their dead; Great Britain, 67 percent; and the United States, 12½ percent. The number of cremations in each country is largely dictated by the cost and availability of burial ground.

THE MANY FACES OF DEATH

According to a 1985 health report, 50 percent of all deaths and illnesses are either unnecessary or premature. After studying the most prevalent causes of death and disease in the United States, the Carter Center at Emory University concluded that a healthy life-style is twice as effective as medical technology at increasing life expectancy.

The number one cause of premature death is cigarette smoking: 360,000 deaths each year are directly attributable to smoking. Most of these deaths occur as heart attacks, strokes, diabetes, cancer, and chronic lung disease. Tobacco is the most deadly carcinogen known, with an estimated 6,000 chemicals—many of which are poisonous—present in cigarette smoke.

Alcohol ranks second to tobacco as a factor in causing death. Deaths related to alcohol total 75,000 per year in the United States, and even higher in the USSR. Of the U.S. deaths, about 20,000 are due to illness; 24,000 are due to motor vehicle accidents; and 32,000 more are due to falls, fires, drownings, homicides, and suicides.

Cholesterol and Premature Death

It is estimated that 80 percent of middle-aged men have a high risk of dying prematurely from heart disease because of excessively high cholesterol levels. The chance of dying from heart disease rises as the amount of cholesterol found in the blood increases. For a person with 182 to 202 milligrams of cholesterol per 100 deciliters of blood, the increased risk of death is 29 percent. From 203 to 220, the risk is 73 percent. And from 221 to 244, the odds skyrocket to 121 percent. As of 1986, the average cholesterol level among middle-aged U.S. men and women was about 215.

According to a 1984 study by the National Heart, Lung, and Blood Institute, every one-percent drop in cholesterol level leads to a two-percent drop in the likelihood of having a heart attack. The occurrence of a heart attack is very rare when cholesterol is less than 150.

Killers at Large

Arteriosclerosis, or clogged arteries, claims more lives worldwide than any other disease. Along with other heart diseases, over 1,000,000 people in the United States die from it each year.

Cancer is known worldwide in its 100 different forms but does not claim as many lives as heart disease nor is it as widespread. Only one group of people anywhere on earth have been found to be totally free of it: the Hunza in northwest Kashmir, a people known for their longevity.

Stroke, a result of a clogged artery leading to the brain, ranks high as a cause of death around the globe, but its fatality rate in the United States has dropped by 32 percent in recent years due to improved medical care.

Malaria, a notorious cause of death in underdeveloped countries, is currently making a dramatic resurgence worldwide. Once thought to be eradicable, tough new resistant strains of the disease are making the travelers' dose of chloroquine virtually useless. According to the World Health Organization, the incidence of malaria has more than quadrupled in the last 10 years. In 1981 there were 151 million new cases of malaria reported. One form of malaria, known as "plasmodium falciparum," kills 40 percent of its victims who remain untreated and is responsible for more than 1 million deaths of African children each year.

Other primary human killers include enteritis; influenza; various lung diseases such as bronchitis, emphysema, and asthma; diabetes; cirrhosis of the liver; and tuberculosis.

Suicide

More than 1,000 people commit suicide worldwide each day.

Country	Number of Male Suicides	Number of Female Suicides
Australia	1,199	408
Chile	460	80
France	7,362	3,044
West Germany	8,743	4,636
Hong Kong	303	216
Hungary	3,293	1,587
Japan	12,708	7,388
Kuwait	7	3
Netherlands	865	566
Sweden	1,137	473
Thailand	1,803	1,655
U.K. (England/Wales)	2,761	1,658
Scotland	364	197
United States	20,256	6,950

*Compiled from 1980 and 1981 figures

For every suicide, there are an estimated 15 unsuccessful suicide attempts. In Hungary in 1981, 1 person in every 1,575 committed suicide, the highest recorded rate in the world. In Kuwait, fewer than 1 in 100,000 people killed themselves in 1981.

Death by Accident

Injuries, meanwhile, kill more people between ages 5 and 44 than all other causes combined. The 8 leading causes of death by injury in the United States in 1986 were motor vehicle (47,900), falls (11,000), drowning (5,600), fire (4,800), choking on food (3,600), accidental firearm shooting (1,800), poisoning (4,000), and poisoning by gas (900).

About 18,000 people in the United States are murdered each year.

The Hepatitis/Cancer Connection

There are an estimated 280 million carriers of hepatitis-B virus worldwide, mostly in developing nations. Of these, 50 million will die of liver cancer, making the virus second only to tobacco as a cause of death by cancer worldwide.

HOW LONG WILL YOU LIVE?

The life-expectancy quiz given below is typical of questionnaires now used by physicians and insurance companies across the nation. Because of the myriad of risk factors involved, such questionnaires are by no means 100 percent accurate. For example, how can one measure the strength of an individual's immune system? A tiny percentage of cigarette smokers, for instance, will live until age 80 or 90, while a nonsmoker may die of lung cancer at age 35. Though exceptions exist to every rule, don't take the quiz too lightly. Odds are that your predicted life span will be quite close.

- **Start with the number 74.**
    If you're male, subtract 2.
    If you're female, add 4.
    If you live in an urban area with a population over 2 million, subtract 2.

If you live in a rural area with a population under 10,000, add 2.

If any grandparent lived to be 85, add 2.

If all four grandparents lived to be 80, add 6.

If either parent died of a stroke or heart attack before the age of 50, subtract 4.

If any immediate relative (parent, brother, sister) under 50 has—or had—cancer or a heart condition, or has had diabetes since childhood, subtract 3.

If you earn over $50,000 a year, subtract 2.

If you finished college, add 1. If you have a graduate or professional degree, add 2 more.

If you live with a spouse or a friend, add 5. If not, subtract 1 for every 10 years alone since age 25.

If you work behind a desk, subtract 3.

If your work is physically demanding, add 3.

If you exercise 3 to 5 times a week for at least 30 minutes, add 4.

If you exercise twice a week, add 2.

If you sleep more than 10 hours per night, subtract 4.

If you are aggressive, tense, or easily angered, subtract 3.

If you are generally relaxed and easygoing, add 3.

If you are generally happy most of the time, add 1.

If you are generally unhappy most of the time, subtract 2.

If you smoke a pack of cigarettes a day, subtract 7.

If you smoke 2 packs or more a day, subtract 8.

If you smoke half-a-pack a day, subtract 3.

If you drink more than 1½ ounces of liquor a day, subtract 1.

If you are overweight by 10 to 30 pounds, subtract 2.

If overweight by 30 to 50 pounds, subtract 4.

If overweight by 50 pounds or more, subtract 8.

If you have an annual physical exam, add 2.
If you are between age 30 and 40, add 2.
If you are between 40 and 50, add 3.
If you are between 50 and 70, add 4.
If you are over 70, add 5.

■ **Add a "plus" sign (+) to your expected life span if any of the following pertain to you.**
    Blood pressure less than 130/75
    Cholesterol less than 200
    Resting pulse rate less than 60 beats per minute
    No breathing problems or asthma
    No history of chronic illness
    Presently live with a pet
    Still working after age 62
    Light eater
    Don't skip breakfast
    Have social contacts besides spouse

All of the above factors enhance life span.

■ **Add a "minus" sign (−) to your expected life span if any of the following pertain to you.**
    Blood pressure greater than 140/90
    Cholesterol greater than 200
    Take a long time to recover after exercise
    Anemic
    Suffer illnesses more than the average person your age
    Easily winded
    Resting pulse rate greater than 80 beats per minute
    Heavy eater
    Skip breakfast
    No social contacts besides spouse

HOW LONG CAN WE LIVE?

Human life spans have increased rapidly in the last century. Our gains in life expectancy are due largely to achievements in preventing and curing disease. Life spans will continue to lengthen as medical science makes new advances. In fact, by the year 2000, men living in modernized nations are projected to survive well into their eighties while women will live into their nineties. For years the maximum human life span was thought to be 110; however, in the near future new anti-aging lifestyles and medical technology now on the horizon promise to shatter this long-supposed biological limit, dramatically extending our life spans.

Fountains of Youth

Our general nutrition helps to determine whether we die younger or live longer. The numbers of deaths from heart disease and some cancers are already declining as people fine tune their diets. Certain vitamins, such as vitamin A, have already been clearly linked to the prevention of some lung and colon cancers, and avoiding saturated fats significantly decreases the rate of heart disease.

Other studies show that undereating in itself may help you live longer. Research on laboratory rats has shown that underfed rats live one-third longer than their well-fed peers. Moreover, this longevity factor appears to work no matter at what age the rat is put on the diet. Scientists believe such low-calorie diets may help humans live longer too.

Life Preservers

Medical science has already enabled us to store blood, sperm, nerves, veins, bones, aortic heart valves, fibrous tissue, cartilage, tendons, skin, marrow, eyes, and dura mater (the outer covering of the brain) for later use. Brain tissue and other higher organs can be stored for several hours for a wide array of medical uses. These storage times are expected to increase as preservation techniques are improved.

As new drugs are developed that suppress the body's rejection of transplanted organs, the replacement of failing organs with healthy ones will be increasingly common. Organ transplantation could very well become the major life-extending technology of the future.

In addition, continued advances in biomedical research may allow millions of us to replace worn-out or damaged body parts with man-made substitutes. Two decades ago artificial organs were only temporary substitutes for natural body functions and were to be used only in emergencies. Today artificial joints, cardiac pacemakers, and lens implants for the eye are virtually permanent replacements that enable their users to live almost normal lives. In the coming years we can expect far better replacement parts to be developed. We may see the emergence of a truly successful artificial heart, a sensitive electronic ear to overcome deafness, or an artificial pancreas that could add years to a diabetes patient's life.

Who knows? In the future, with advancements in surgery and transplant technology, you may even be able to have an off-the-shelf compass in your nose.

Good luck.